Kid's Box

Updated Second Edition

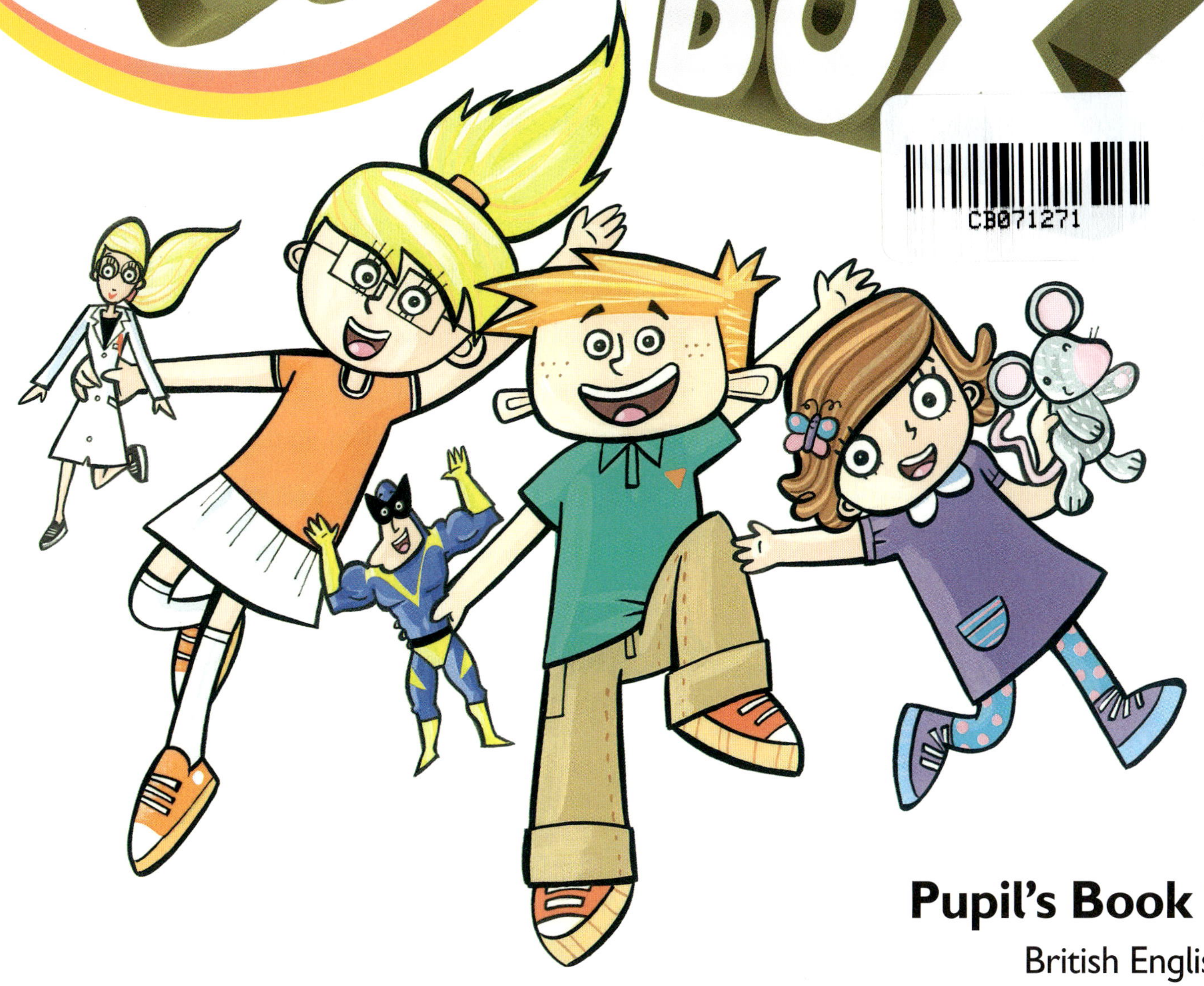

Pupil's Book 2
British English

Caroline Nixon & Michael Tomlinson

Language summary

	Key vocabulary	Key grammar and functions	Phonics
1 Hello again! page 4	**Character names:** Mr Star, Mrs Star, Stella, Simon, Suzy, Grandma Star, Grandpa Star, Marie, Maskman, Monty, Trevor **Numbers:** 1-10 **Colours:** red, yellow, pink, green, orange, blue, purple, brown, black, white, grey	**Greetings:** Hello, we're the Star family. Who's he/she? This is my brother, Simon. He's seven, and this is my sister, Suzy. She's four. **Prepositions:** in, on, under	Long vowel sound: 'ay' (pl<u>ay</u>)
2 Back to school page 10	**Character names:** Alex, Lenny, Meera **School:** bookcase, board, cupboard, computer, desk, ruler, teacher, television, whiteboard **Numbers:** 11-20	How many (books) are there? There are/aren't (ten desks). Is there (a ruler) on the (desk)? Yes, there is./No there isn't. Are there (ten pens) on the (desk)? Yes, there are./No, there aren't. **Prepositions:** next to	Long vowel sound: 'ee' (thr<u>ee</u>)

Marie's maths · **Block graphs** page 16 **Trevor's values** · **Be polite** page 17

3 Play time! page 18	**Toys:** alien, camera, computer game, kite, lorry, robot, watch	this, that, these, those Whose is this (bag)? It's Tom's. Whose are these (shoes)? They're Sue's.	Long vowel sound: 'i' (f<u>i</u>ve, fl<u>y</u>)
4 At home page 24	**Furniture:** bath, bed, clock, lamp, mat, mirror, phone, sofa	It's mine. It's yours. Is that hat yours? Yes, it is./No, it isn't. Are those blue socks yours? Yes, they are./No, they aren't.	Long vowel sound: 'oa/o_e' (b<u>oa</u>t, ph<u>o</u>n<u>e</u>)

Marie's art · **Origami** page 30 **Trevor's values** · **Re-use and recycle** page 31

Review  page 32

5 Meet my family page 34	**Character names:** Tony, Alice, Nick, Kim, Hugo, Lucy, May, Lenny, Sam, Frank **Family:** baby, cousin, mum, dad, grandma, grandpa	What are you doing? I'm reading. What's Grandpa doing? He's sleeping. **Verb + -ing spellings:** hitting, running, sitting, swimming **Verbs:** catch, clean, fly, get, hit, jump, kick, run, sit, sleep, talk, throw	Long vowel sound: 'oo' (bl<u>ue</u>, r<u>u</u>ler)
6 Dinner time page 40	**Food:** bread, chicken, chips, eggs, juice, milk, rice, water	Can I have some (egg and chips)? Here you are.	Consonant sound: 'ch' (<u>ch</u>icken)

Marie's science · **Food** page 46 **Trevor's values** · **Eat good food** page 47

		Key vocabulary	Key grammar and functions	Phonics
7	**At the farm** page 48	**Animals:** cow, duck, frog, goat, lizard, sheep, spider	I love (horses). So do I. / I don't.	Initial letter blends: 'sp' and 'st' (<u>sp</u>ider, <u>st</u>ar)
8	**My town** page 54	**Places:** café, flat, hospital, park, shop, street	Where's the blue car? It's in front of the shop. It's between the red car and the grey car. **Prepositions:** behind, between, in front of, next to	Vowel sound: 'ow' (br<u>ow</u>n, m<u>ou</u>se)

Marie's music | **Animals in music** — page 60

Trevor's values | **Your town** — page 61

Review 5 6 7 8 — page 62

9	**Our clothes** page 64	**Clothes:** dress, glasses, handbag, hat, jeans, shirt, sunglasses	He/She's wearing (a blue T-shirt) and (white shoes). They're wearing (sunglasses) and (big red hats). have/has got	Consonant sounds: 's' and 'sh' (<u>s</u>even, <u>sh</u>eep)
10	**Our hobbies** page 70	**Activities:** paint, play badminton / baseball / basketball / hockey / table tennis	I like painting. I love playing hockey. I don't like playing the guitar. Do you like reading? Yes, I do. / No, I don't.	Final consonant blend: 'ng' (si<u>ng</u>)

Marie's maths | **Venn diagrams** — page 76

Trevor's values | **Sports rules** — page 77

11	**My birthday** page 78	**Food:** burger, cake, fries, lemonade, orange, sausage, watermelon	Would you like (some fries)? Yes, please. / No, thank you. Can I have (some lemonade)? Here you are.	Long vowel sound: 'ir / ur' (b<u>ir</u>thday, p<u>ur</u>ple)
12	**On holiday!** page 84	**Places:** beach, mountain, sand, sea, shell, sun	Where do you want to go on holiday? I want to go to the beach. I don't want to go to a big city.	Short vowel sounds: 'a', 'e', 'i', 'o', 'u' (D<u>a</u>d, B<u>e</u>n, J<u>i</u>ll, T<u>o</u>m, M<u>u</u>m)

Marie's geography | **Maps** — page 90

Trevor's values | **Helping holidays** — page 91

Review 9 10 11 12 — page 92

Grammar reference — page 94

5 Listen, point and repeat.

a b c d
e f g
h i j k
l m n o p
q r s
t u v
w x y z

6 Say the chant.

7 💬 Ask and answer.

pink grey green orange red brown white blue yellow black purple

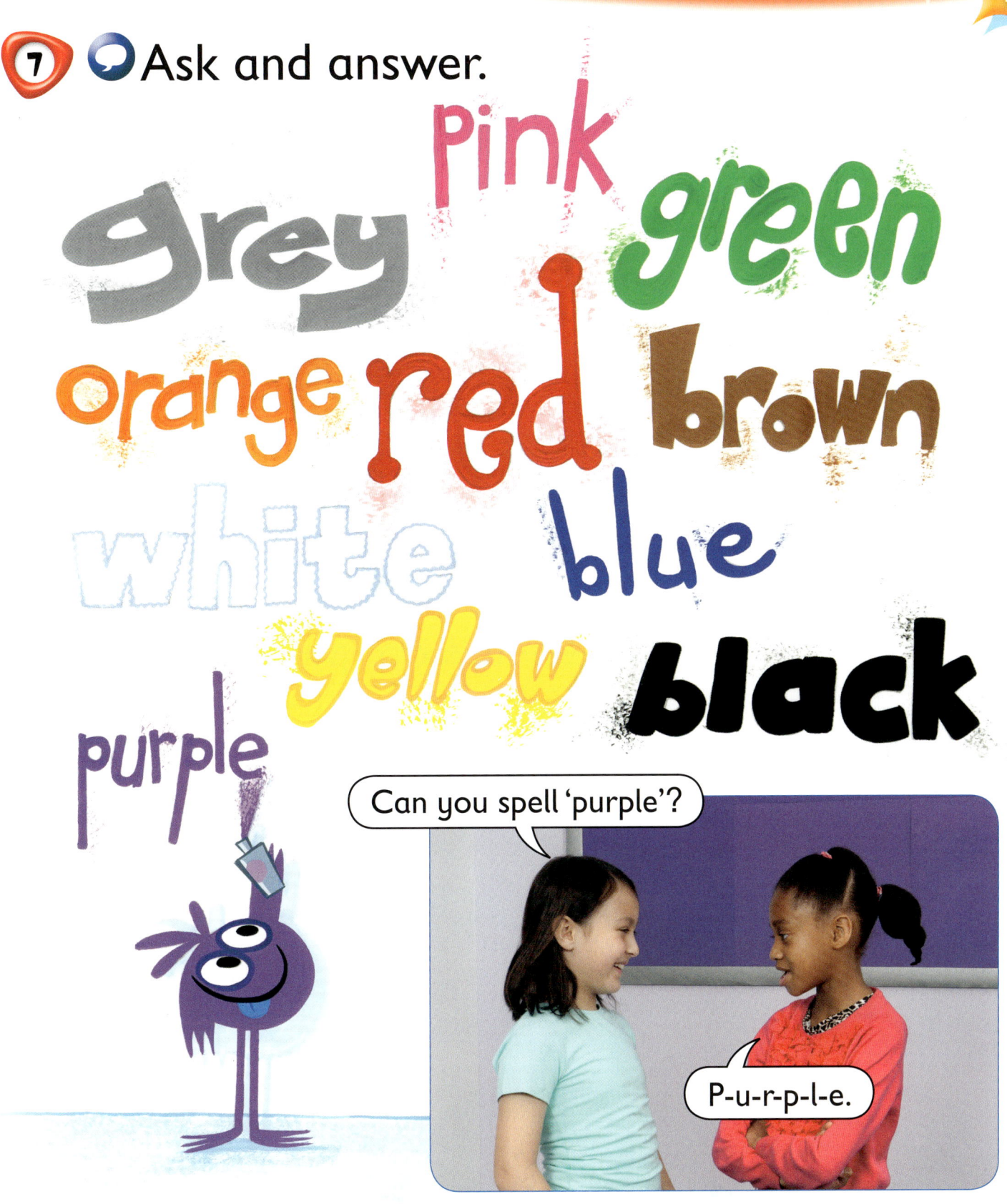

Can you spell 'purple'?

P-u-r-p-l-e.

8 💬 Order the colours.　　Black, blue, brown …

9 10 CD1 Monty's phonics

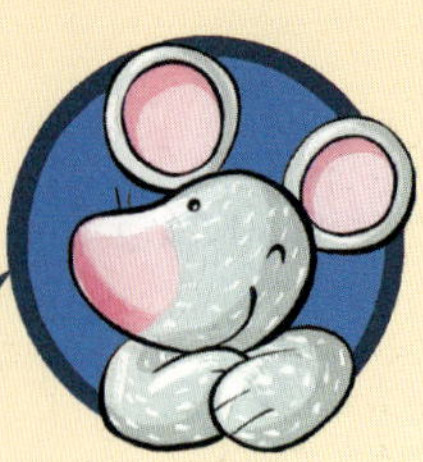

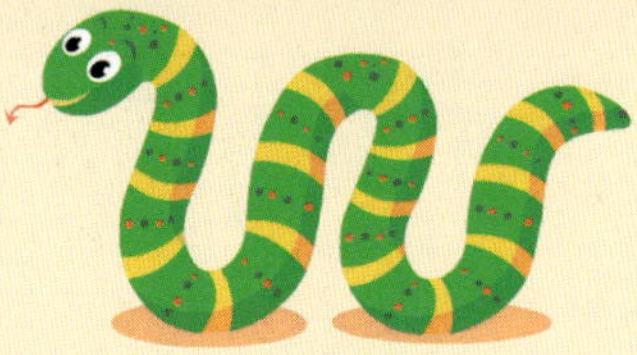

snake

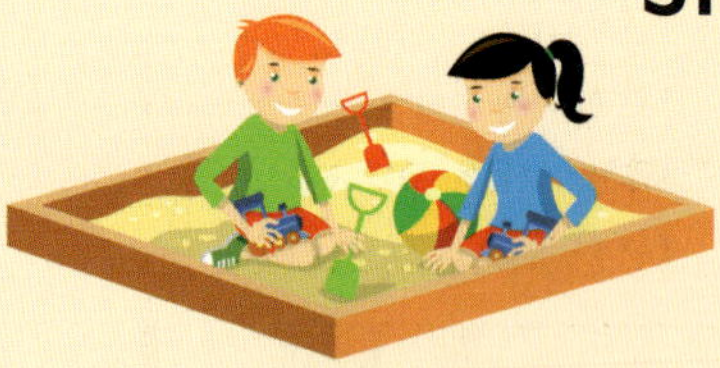

play

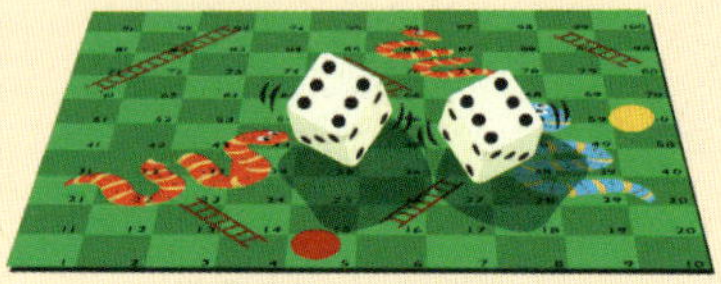

game

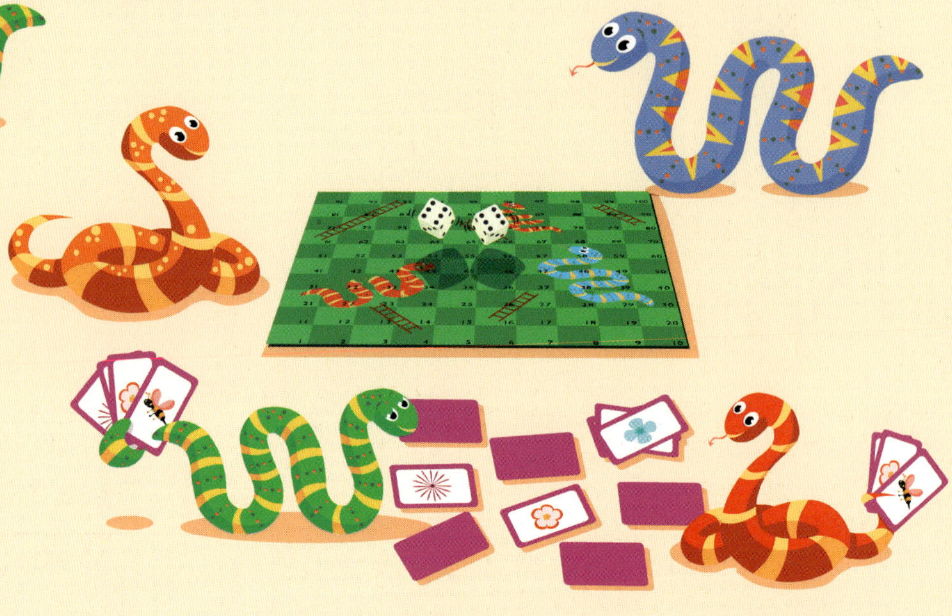

Four snakes are playing games!

10 Say and answer.

The pencil is under the chair.
That's h.

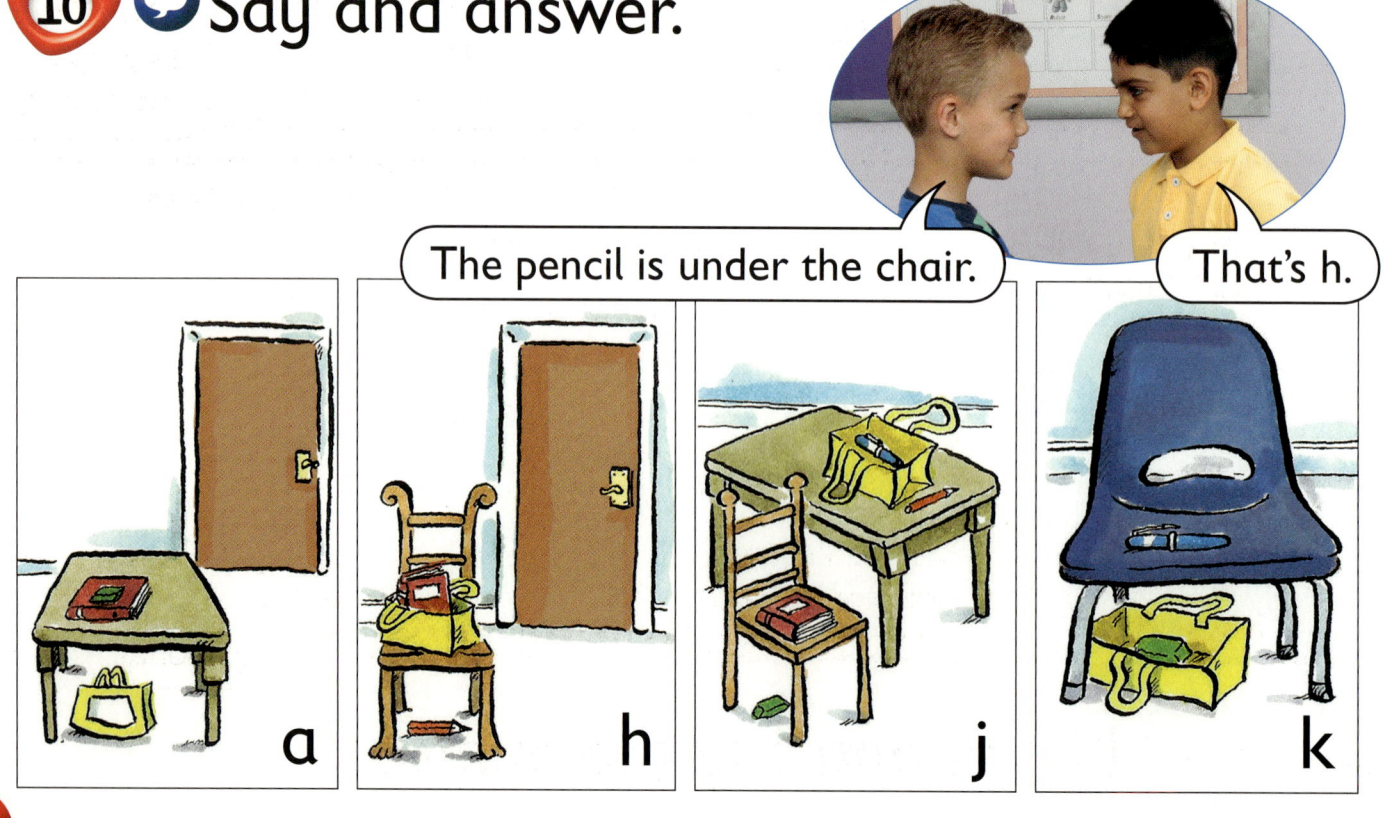

a

h

j

k

 Listen to the story.

  Listen and say the number.

2 Back to school

1) 🎧 Listen and point.

2) 🎧 💬 Listen and repeat.

③   Listen and point. Chant.

School, school. This is the Numbers School.
11   Eleven desks,
12   Twelve erasers,
13   Thirteen rulers,
14   Fourteen cupboards,
15   Fifteen classrooms,
16   Sixteen teachers,
17   Seventeen pens,
18   Eighteen boards,
19   Nineteen pencils,
20   Twenty tables.
School, school. This is the Numbers School.

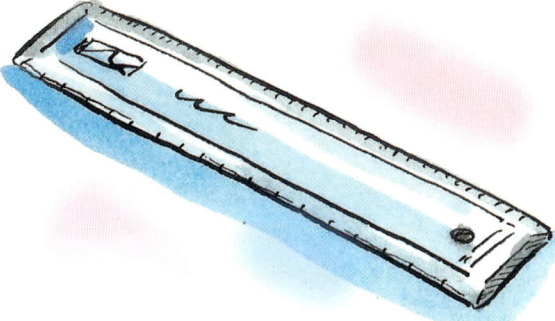

④  Ask and answer.

How many desks are there?   11

Vocabulary
board   bookcase   cupboard   desk   ruler   teacher

5 Listen and point.

CD1 20

This is my classroom. How many desks are there? There are a lot of desks. That's my desk next to the bookcase. There's a long pink ruler on it. There are a lot of books in the bookcase. There's a big whiteboard on the wall. There's a computer, but there isn't a television.

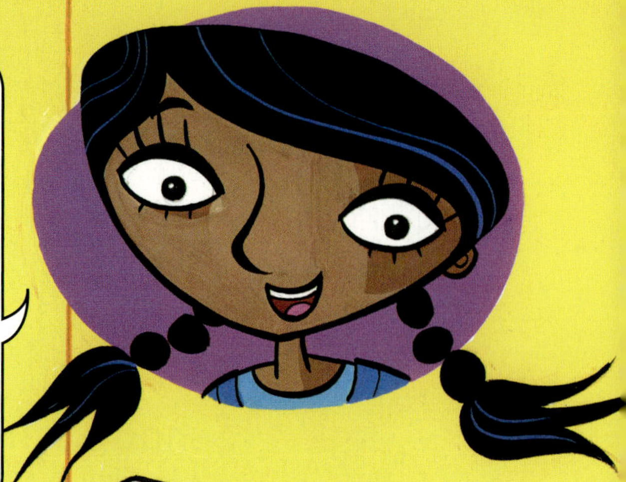

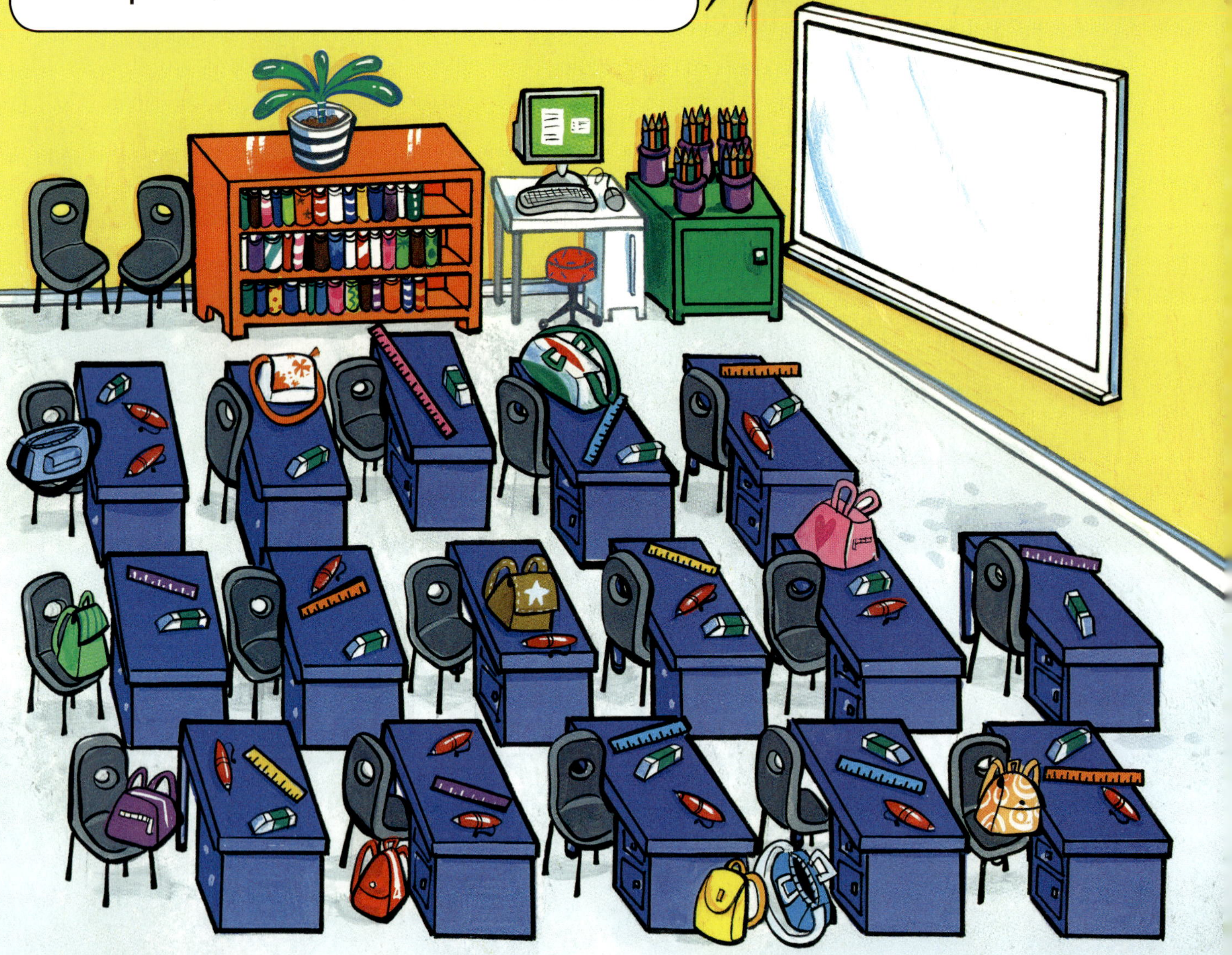

6 Listen and repeat.

CD1 21

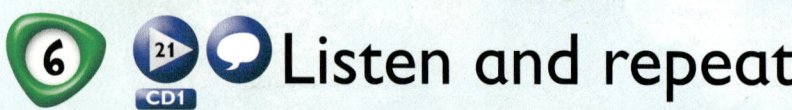

Grammar

How many … are there? There is … There are …

7   Listen and point. Sing.

There are pencils in the classroom, yes there are.
There's a cupboard on the pencils, yes there is.
There's a ruler on the cupboard,
There's a bookcase on the ruler,
There's a teacher on the bookcase, yes there is …

8  Ask and answer.

(Where's the cupboard?) (On the pencils.)

9 Monty's phonics

3 three

teacher

tree

Three teachers sleeping in a tree!

10 Say and correct.

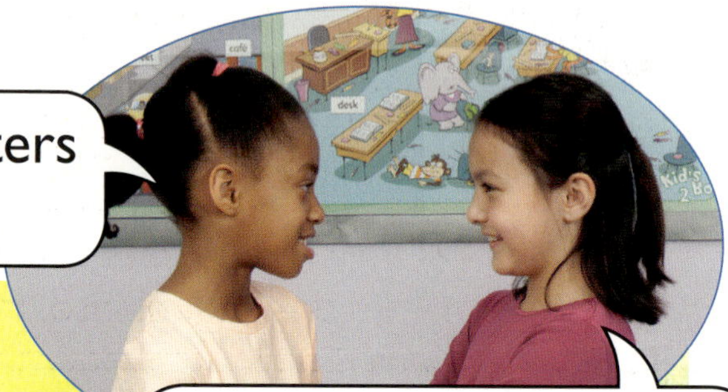

"There are three posters in the classroom."

"No, there aren't. There are two posters."

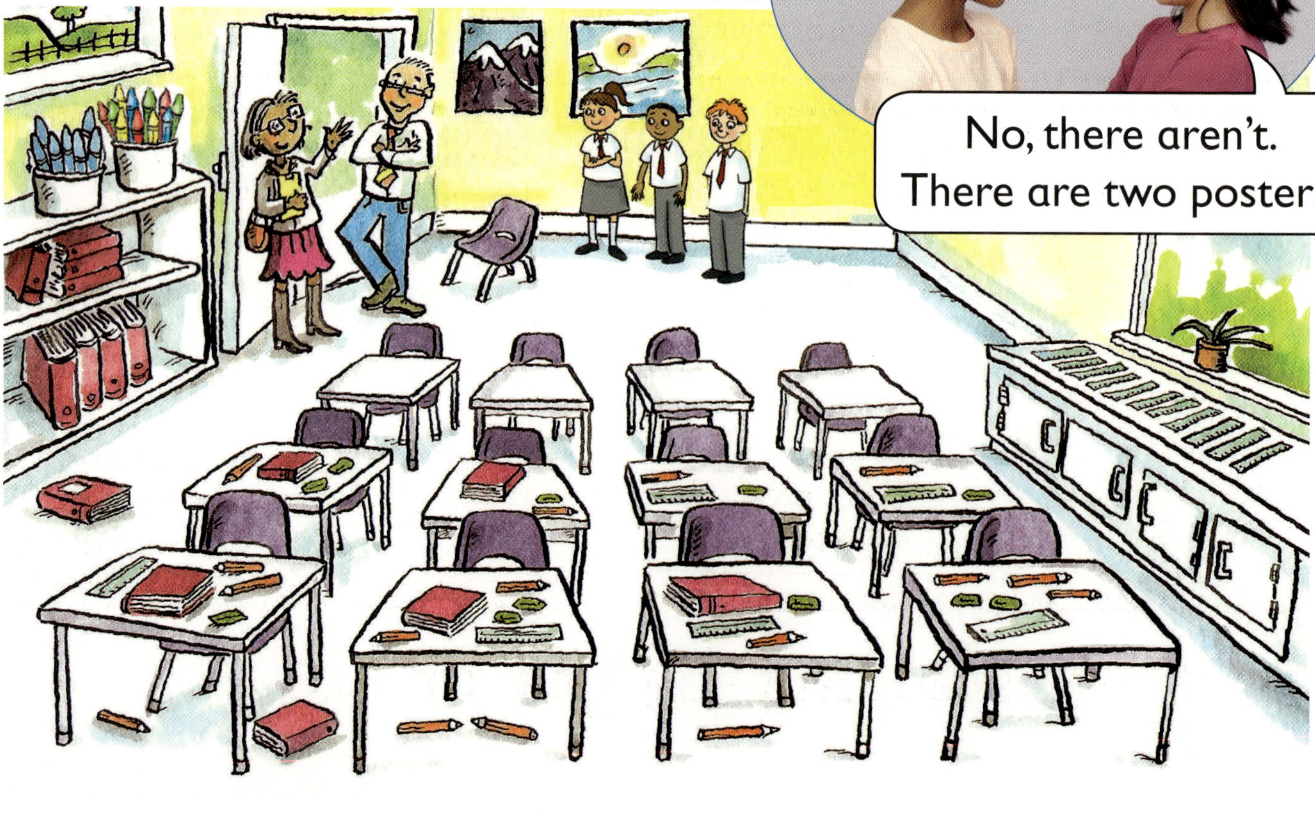

 Listen to the story.

  Listen and say 'yes' or 'no'.

Marie's maths — Block graphs

1 🎧 CD1 28 👂 Listen and point.

orange　banana　apple　pear　pineapple　lemon

2 🎧 CD1 29 💬 Listen and answer.

oranges　bananas　apples　pears　pineapples　lemons

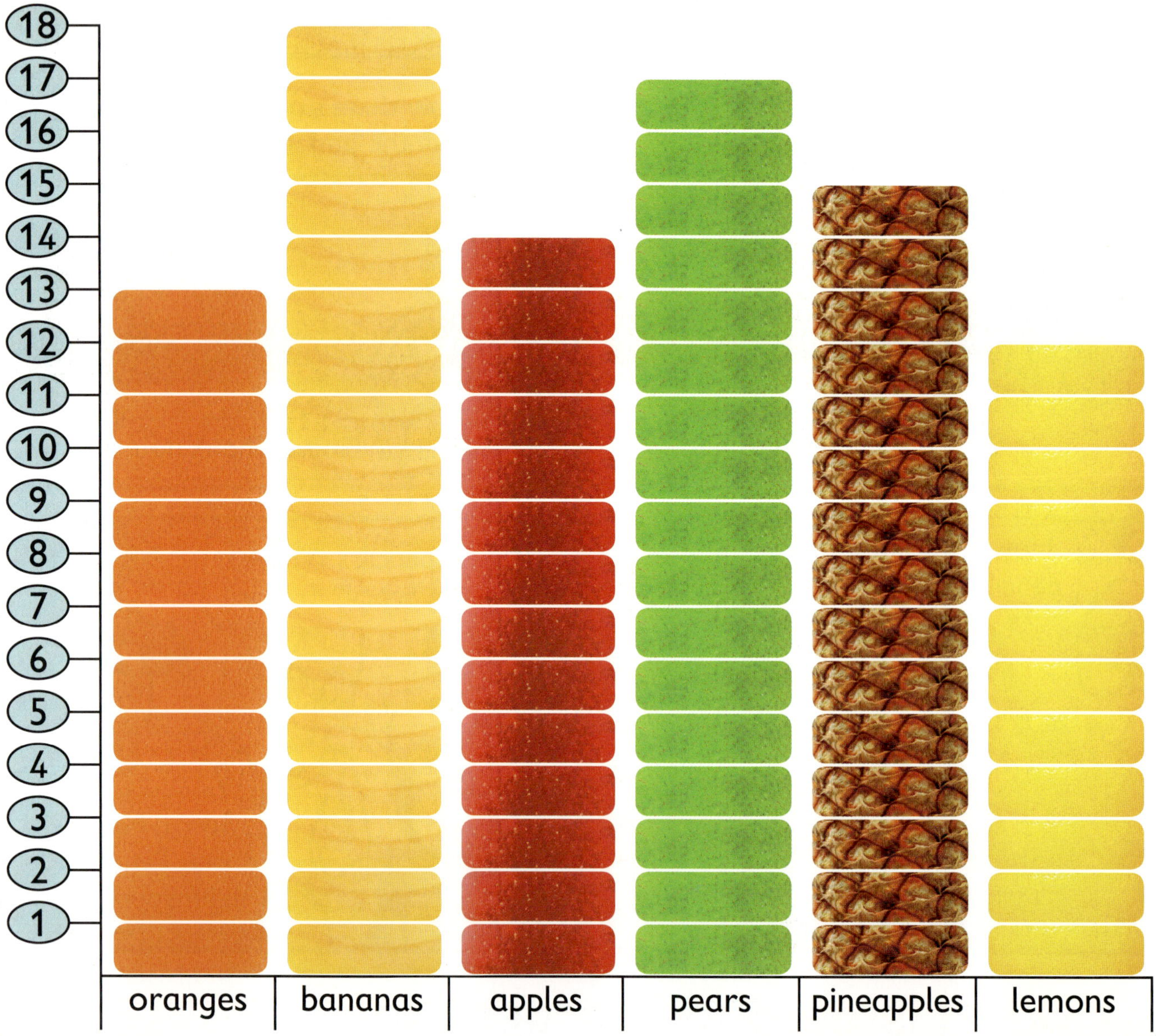

Vocabulary: lemon　pear　pineapple

Now you! Activity Book page 16

16

Be polite — Trevor's values

3   Listen and say the number.

4 Act it out.

Functions

After you. Thank you. Can you … please? Yes, of course.
Can we come in? Yes, come in.

3 [CD1 34] Listen and say the number.

"These are dolls." 19. "This is a robot." 17.

4 [CD1 35] Listen and say 'yes' or 'no'.

Vocabulary
alien camera computer game kite lorry robot watch

Grammar
this these

19

5   Listen and point.

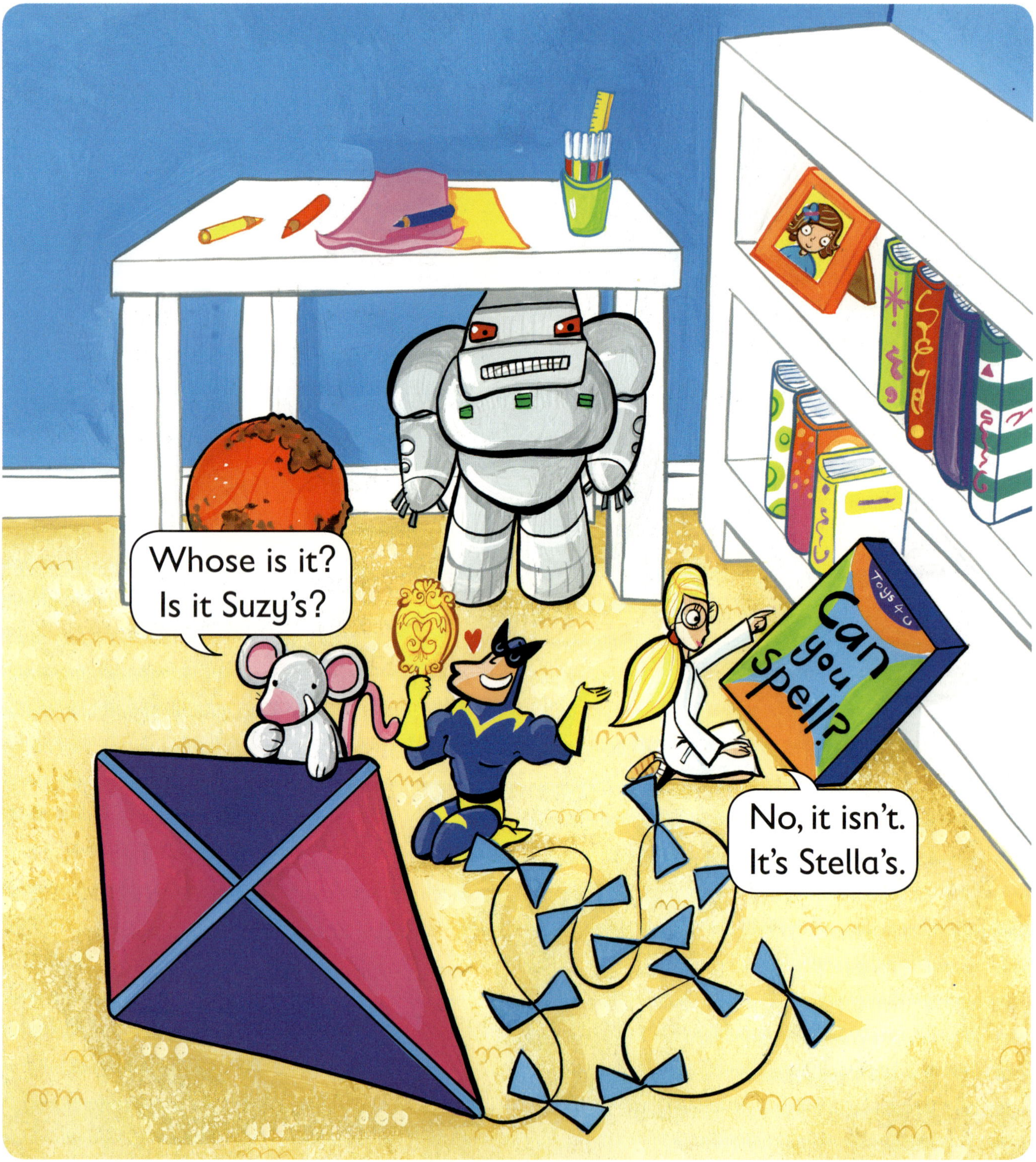

6   Listen and repeat.

Grammar
Whose is this? Whose are these?

7 🎵 Listen and point. Sing.

Whose is this jacket? ...
What? That black jacket?
Yes, this black jacket.
Whose is this jacket?
It's John's.
Oh!

Whose are these shoes? ...
What? Those blue shoes?
Yes, these blue shoes.
Whose are these shoes?
They're Sheila's.
Oh!

Whose is this skirt? ...
What? That purple skirt?
Yes, this purple skirt.
Whose is this skirt?
It's Sue's.
Oh!

Whose are these trousers? ...
What? Those brown trousers?
Yes, these brown trousers.
Whose are these trousers?
They're Tom's.
Oh!

8 💬 Ask and answer.

(Whose are these trousers?)   (They're Tom's.)

9 Monty's phonics

fly

five

kite

I'm flying my five white kites.

10 Ask and answer.

11. Whose is this nose? — It's Simon's.

12. Whose are these eyes? — They're Stella's.

 Listen to the story.

 Act out the story.

4 At home

1 **Listen and point.**

2 **Listen and repeat.**

3  Listen and point. Chant.

There's a mirror in the bathroom,
And a phone in the hall.
A sofa in the living room,
A clock on the wall.
There's a lamp on the table,
And a mat next to the bed.
There's a boat in the bath,
And the boat is red.

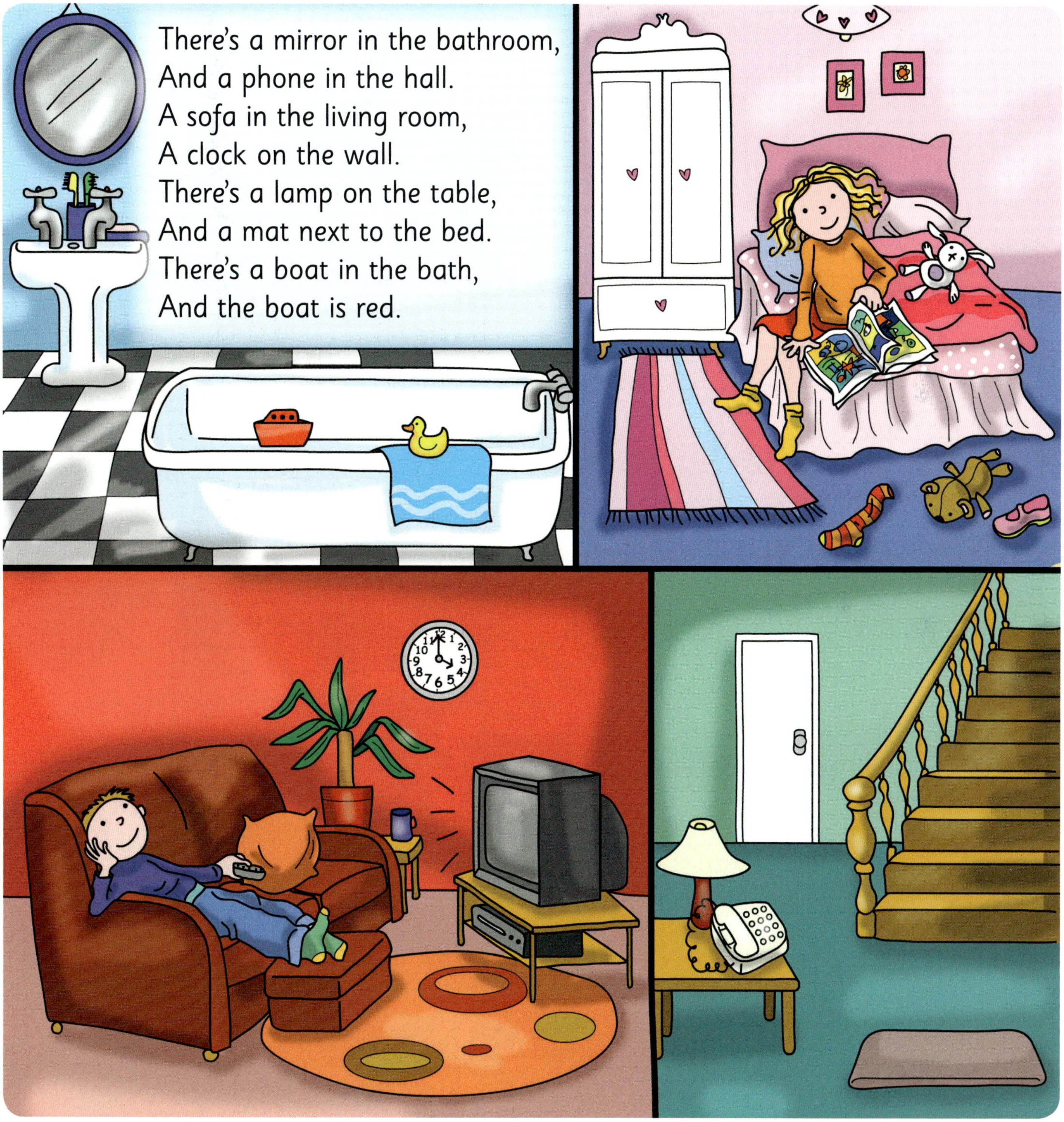

4  Listen and correct.

There's a boy sitting on the sofa.

Vocabulary

clock   lamp   mat   mirror   phone   sofa

5   Listen and point.

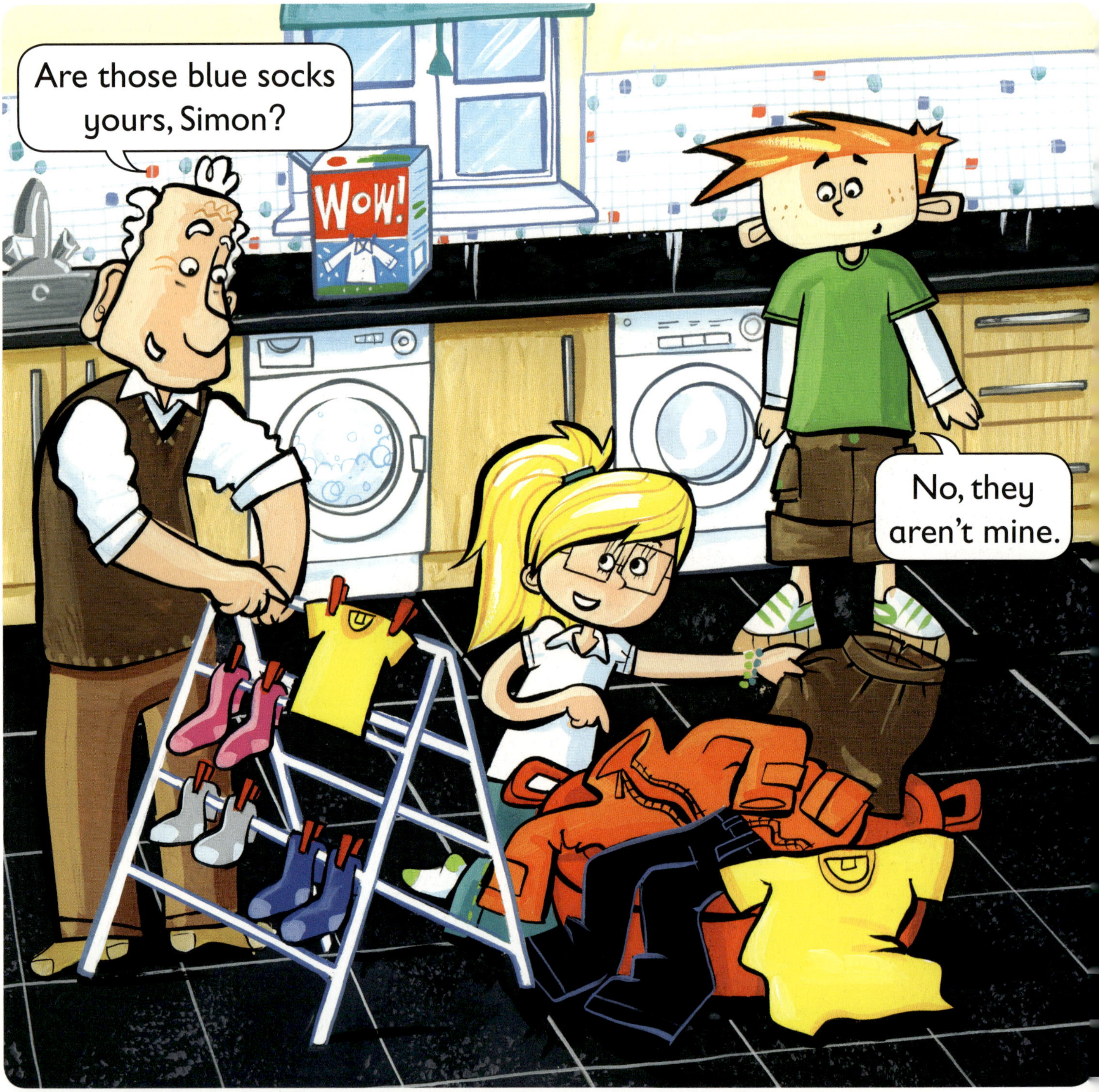

6   Listen and repeat.

Grammar
It's mine / yours.

7   Listen and point. Sing.

Look at this!
Look at this!

Whose are these shoes? ...
Stella! Are they yours? ...
No, they aren't mine! ...

Hmm. Which shoes are Simon's? ...
Which, which, which, which?
Which shoes are Simon's?
The grey ones are his ...

Hmm. Which shoes are Suzy's? ...
Which, which, which, which?
Which shoes are Suzy's?
The red ones are hers ...

SO! Whose shoes are those? ...
Whose, whose, whose, whose?
Whose shoes are those?
Those are Grandpa's ...
Grandpa's?

GRANDPA!

8  Ask and answer.

Which bag is yours?   The red one's mine.

9 Monty's phonics

ph**one**

yell**ow**

b**oa**t

A ph**one** in a yell**ow** b**oa**t!

10 Find your partner.

Are these trousers yours or mine?

They're mine.

11  Listen to the story.

12   Listen and say the number.

Marie's art — Origami

1 🔊 💬 Listen and say.

"What is it?" "It's a kite."

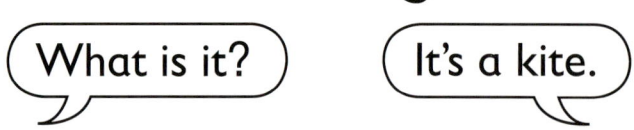

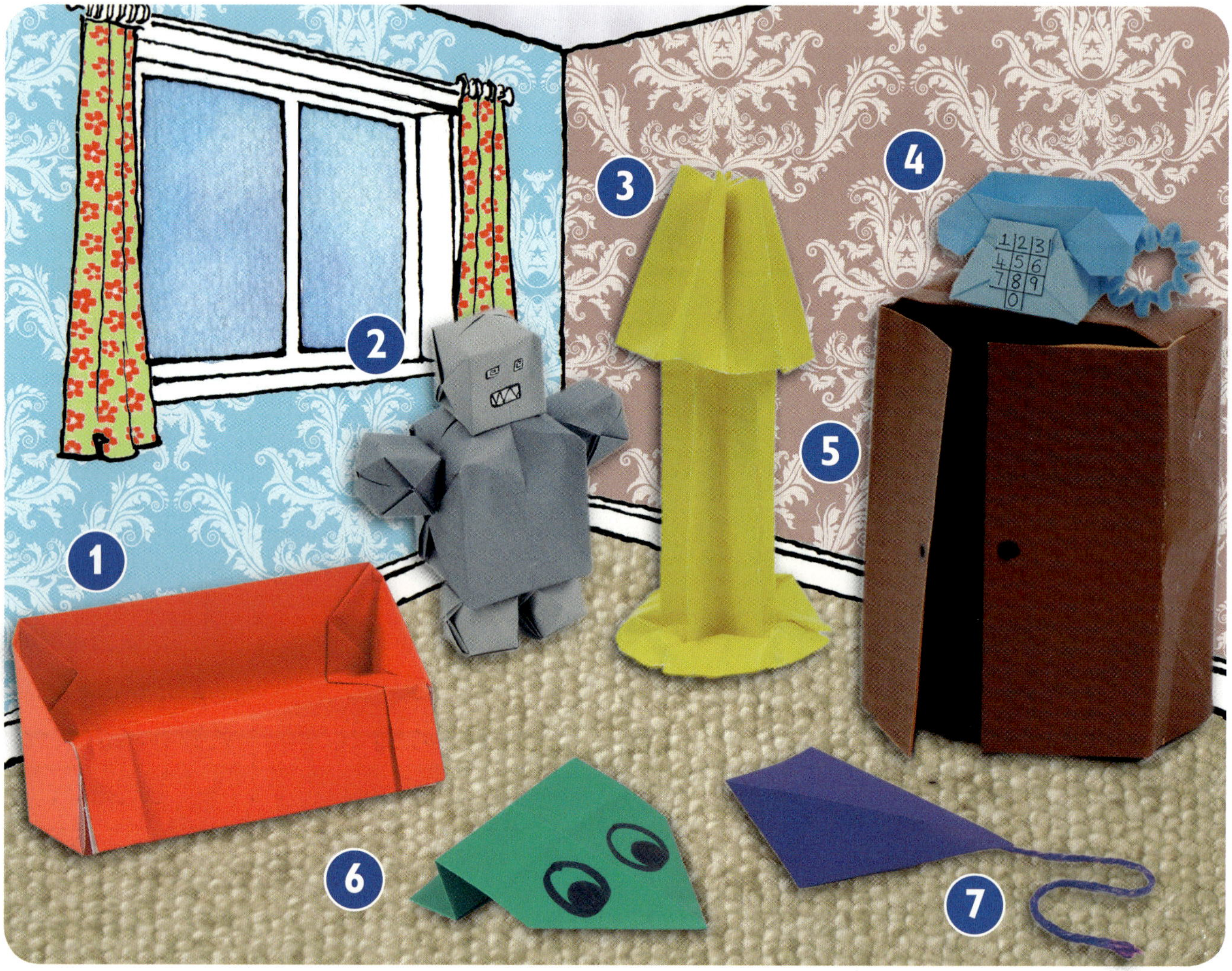

2 🔍 💬 What do you think this is?

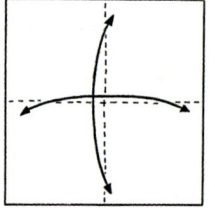 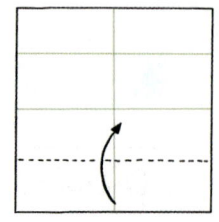 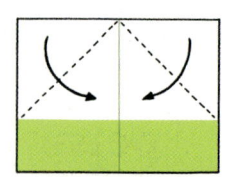 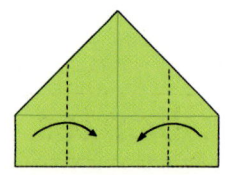

Now you!
Activity Book page 30

Re-use and recycle — Trevor's values

3   Listen and say the number.

1 2 3 4

4 🔍💬 Ask and answer.

- What's this?
- It's a flowerpot.
- What's it made from?
- It's made from a boot.

5 💬 What do you re-use at home?

bottles

paper

plastic bags

I re-use ... at home.

Vocabulary: bottle flowerpot keyboard paper plastic bag

31

Review

1. 🎧 💬 Listen and say the number.

2. 🔍 💬 Look and say.

In picture one there's a purple mat on the floor, but in picture two there's a purple rug on the floor.

3 Play the game. Ask and answer.

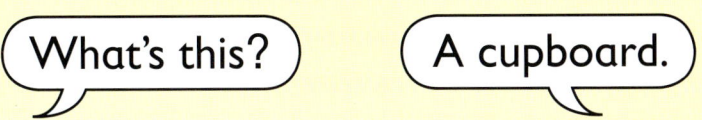

What's this? A cupboard.

5 Meet my family

1. Listen and point.

2. Listen and repeat.

3  Listen and answer.

Tony Alice

Nick Kim Hugo Lucy

May Lenny Sam Frank

4 Look and say.

He's Lenny's father.
Nick.
She's Hugo's mother.
Alice.

Vocabulary
baby   cousin   mum   dad   grandma   grandpa

5 Listen and say the number.

6 Make sentences. Use the words in the box.

The dog's getting the ball.

| getting | throwing | catching | flying | talking | jumping |
| sitting | hitting | cleaning | running | kicking | sleeping |

Grammar
He's / She's... ...ing

Vocabulary
catch clean fly get hit jump run sleep throw

7 🎵 Listen and point. Sing.

My grandpa isn't walking,
He's flying my favourite kite.
My grandma's cleaning the table,
It's beautiful and white.
My father's playing baseball,
He can catch and he can hit.
My cousin's got the ball now,
And now he's throwing it.

My baby sister's sleeping,
She is very small.
My brother isn't jumping,
He's kicking his football.
Hey!

My grandpa isn't walking,
He's flying my favourite kite.
My grandma's cleaning the table,
It's beautiful and white.
My mother's sitting reading,
Her book is big and grey.
And me? I'm very happy,
I can run and play …

8 💬 Ask and answer.

(What's Grandpa doing?)   (He's flying a kite.)

9 Monty's phonics

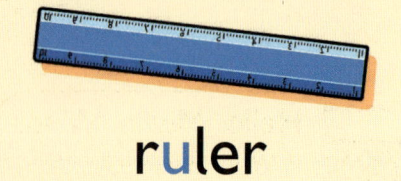

blue

ruler

Sue

Sue's got a big blue ruler!

10 Ask and answer.

What's Simon doing?

He's sleeping.

11 **Listen to the story.**

1. Ooh! What's he doing to those shoes, Marie?
   He's cleaning them, Trevor.

2. Hello, Trevor! Look at me! I'm driving Suzy's yellow lorry.

3. Hello, Maskman. What are you doing?
   I'm flying my helicopter. I'm a superhero.

4. Hello, Marie. What are you doing?
   I'm cleaning my shoes.

5. What are you doing, Trevor?
   I'm cleaning the doll's house.

6. Oh no!

12 **Listen and say the number.**

6 Dinner time

1 🎧 CD2 19 💬 Listen and point.

- bread
- rice
- eggs
- milk
- chips
- juice
- chicken
- water

2 🎧 CD2 20 💬 Listen and repeat.

3 🎵 Listen and point. Sing.

It's morning, it's morning.
We're having breakfast with our mum.
Bread and milk, bread and milk.
It's morning, it's morning.

It's lunchtime, it's lunchtime.
We're having lunch with our friends.
Egg and chips, egg and chips.
It's lunchtime, it's lunchtime.

It's afternoon, it's afternoon.
We're having tea in the garden.
Chocolate cake, chocolate cake.
We're having tea in the afternoon.

It's evening, it's evening.
We're having dinner with Mum and Dad.
Chicken and rice, chicken and rice.
It's evening, it's evening ...

4 👂💬 Point, ask and answer.

(What's this?) (It's chocolate cake.) (What are these?) (They're chips.)

Vocabulary

bread   chicken   chips   eggs   juice   milk   rice   water

5 🎧 CD2 23 💬 Listen and answer.

"Can I have some brown bread, please?"

"Here you are."

6 🎧 CD2 24 💬 Listen and repeat.

Grammar
Can I have some … ? Here you are.

7 Play bingo.

8 Read and answer.

Hello. My name's Alex. I'm Simon's friend. It's lunchtime and I'm having 🐟 and 🍟 for lunch. 🐟 isn't my favourite lunch. My favourite lunch is 🍫.

In the morning my favourite breakfast is 🍎 and 🥛, and my favourite dinner is 🥩 and 🍚.

1 What's his favourite breakfast?

2 What's his favourite lunch?

3 What's his favourite dinner?

9 Monty's phonics

chicken

kitchen

The **ch**ickens are cooking in the ki**tch**en!

10 Ask and answer.

Can I have some bread, please?

Here you are.

11 🔊 Listen to the story.

1. I'm having tomatoes and carrots.

2. Can I have some apple juice, please?

3. Here you are. Is there any chocolate cake?

4. No, there isn't, but there's some chocolate ice cream.

5. Is this orange juice yours, Monty? No, it isn't mine. It's Marie's.

6. What are you eating, Trevor? Is it chicken? Er, no. It isn't chicken. It's a long brown pencil. Oh, Trevor!

12 🔊 💬 Listen and say 'yes' or 'no'.

Marie's science — Food

1 🔍💬 **Look and say.**

Where is milk from?

Animals.

animals

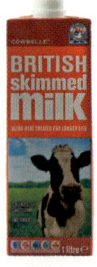

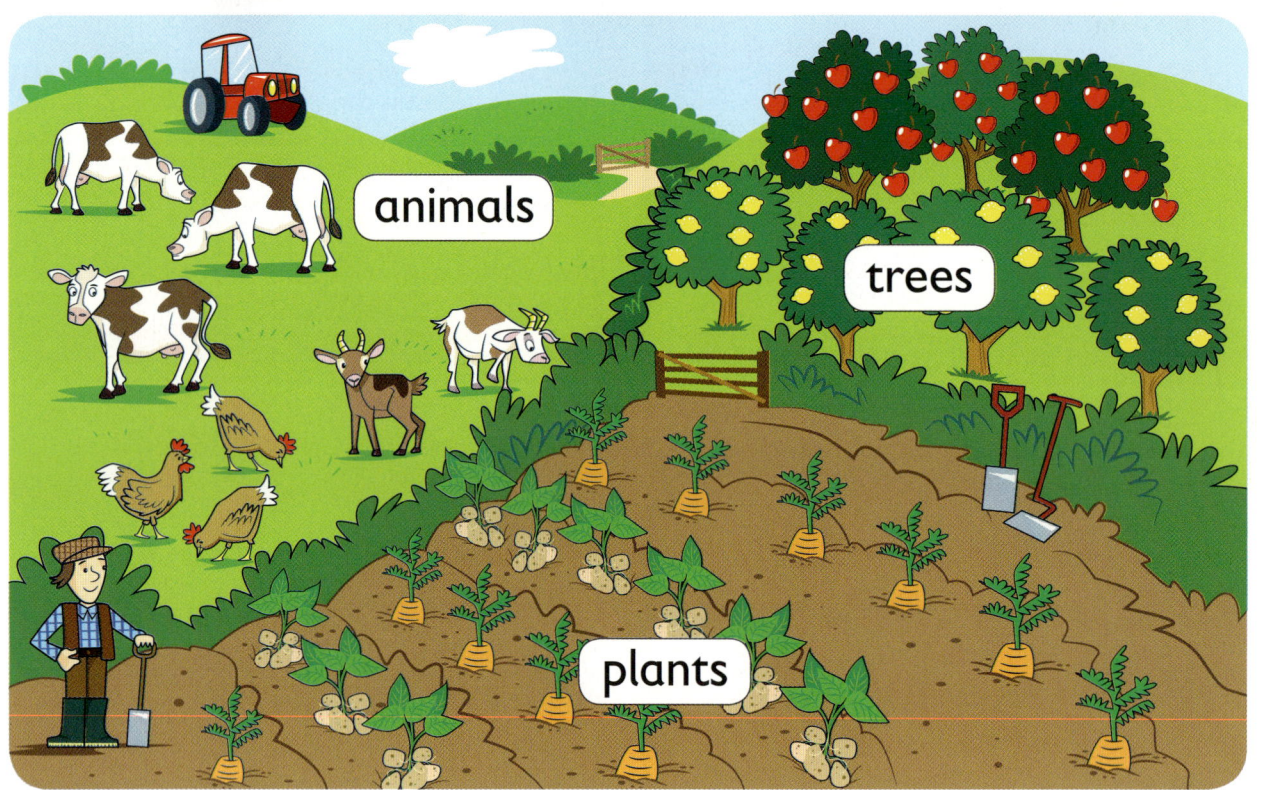

trees

plants

2 🎧💬 **Listen and correct.**

Eggs are from trees.

No, eggs are from animals.

Vocabulary: meat   plant   tree

Now you!
Activity Book page 46

Eat good food — Trevor's values

3 🎵 CD2 31 💬 Listen and say the number.

Breakfast

1

2

Lunch

3

4

Dinner

5

6

4 💬 Ask and answer.

What's number one?

It's a bad breakfast.

What's number four?

It's a good lunch.

47

7 At the farm

1 🎵 32 CD2 💬 Listen and point.

sheep
cow
spider
goat
duck
lizard
frog

Entry

2 🎵 33 CD2 💬 Listen and repeat.

3 🎵 Listen and point. Sing.

Cows in the kitchen, moo moo moo,
Cows in the kitchen.
There are cows in the kitchen, moo moo moo,
What can we do, John Farmer?

Sheep in the bedroom, baa baa baa …

Ducks on the armchair, quack quack quack …

Frogs in the bathroom, croak croak croak …

Chickens in the cupboard, cluck cluck cluck …

4 💬 Ask and answer.

Where are the cows?   In the kitchen.

Vocabulary
cow   duck   frog   goat   lizard   sheep   spider

5 🎧 💬 Listen and answer.

I love horses.

So do I.

I don't.

6 🎧 💬 Listen and repeat.

Grammar
I love ... So do I. I don't.

7 Listen and point. Chant.

I love watermelon.	So do I.
I love pineapple.	So do I.
I love bananas.	So do I.
I love oranges.	So do I.
I love mangoes.	So do I.
I love coconuts.	So do I.
I love lemon and lime.	Hmm. So do I.
I love onions.	I don't. Goodbye.

8 Say and answer.

I love cats. So do I. I love mice. I don't.

9 Monty's phonics

spider

sports

star

The spiders are sports stars!

10 Say and answer.

They're big and grey. They've got long ears.

Donkeys.

11 **Listen to the story.**

1. Trevor! Pssst! Are you sleeping?
   Yes, I am.

2. Trevor! Maskman! Can you be quiet, please? I'm trying to sleep!

3. I can't sleep.
   Well, count sheep, Maskman.

4. 11, 12, 13 … Oh, no! My sheep aren't sleeping. They're jumping! I can't sleep.
   We can't sleep now!

5. OK, let's talk about farms. Farm dogs can get sheep. Farm cats can catch mice. And we get milk from cows.
   Yes … yes, I know. Maskman!

6. What are you doing, Maskman?
   I'm sleeping, Marie. Goodnight.

12 **Act out the story.**

8 My town

1 🎧 45 CD2 💬 **Listen and point.**

flat · park · shop · hospital · café · street

2 🎧 46 CD2 💬 **Listen and repeat.**

3 🔍💬 **Read and answer.**

1. Where's the woman with the baby?
2. How many pineapples are there?
3. How many cats are there?
4. Where's the boy with the kite?
5. What colour are the boots in the shoe shop?
6. Where are the lemons?
7. What colour's the bus?

4 🔍💬 **Ask, count and answer.**

How many skateboards are there?　　There are two skateboards.

skateboards　cars　men　women　children
dogs　babies　pineapples　coconuts　lemons　cats　pets

Vocabulary

café　flat　hospital　park　shop　street

55

5 🔊 Listen and point.

Lenny's mum's in front of me.

6 💬 Ask and answer.

Who's next to Grandma?

Grandpa.

Grammar
behind   between   in front of   next to

7 🎵 Listen and point. Sing.

Put two books on the table …
Put a pencil between the books …
Put a pencil behind your head …
Put a book in front of your nose …
Put a book under your chair …
Put a pencil behind your ear …
Put two books on your head …
Put them all back on the table,
And now, now, sit down.

8 💬 Ask and answer.

Where's the blue book?

On the sofa.

9 Monty's phonics

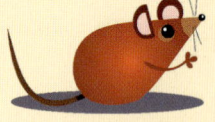

br**ow**n

m**ou**se

h**ou**se

A br**ow**n m**ou**se in a t**ow**n h**ou**se.

10 Ask and answer.

Where's the car?

It's in front of the toy shop.

11 🔊 53 CD2 Listen to the story.

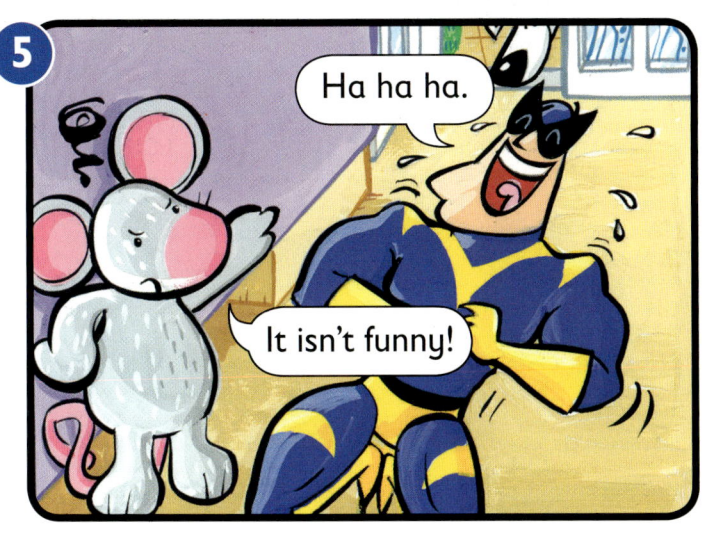

1
— Aaagh! Look behind you. It's behind you!
— Ooooh! I can't look!

2
— Oh, no. It's 'Dogzilla', the monster dog.

3
— I'm coming, children.
— Maskman's our superhero.

4
— Aaagh! Monty! Look behind you. There's a cat. It's 'Catzilla'!
— Eeeek! Help! A cat!

5
— Ha ha ha.
— It isn't funny!

6
— Look! There's a dog. It's behind you.
— Eeeek! Help! There's a dog. It's 'Dogzilla'! Help!

12 🔊 54 CD2 💬 Listen and say the number.

Marie's music — Animals in music

1 🔍💬 Look and say.   *What's this?*   *It's a snake.*

| a frog   a spider   a fish   a bird   a snake   a horse |

1.
2. 
3. 
4. 
5. 
6. 

2 🔊💬 Listen and say the animal.

Now you!
Activity Book page 60

Your town — Trevor's values

3 🎧 💬 Listen and say the number.

1.
2.
3.
4.

Do not walk on the grass

4 🔍 💬 Ask and answer.

(Don't drop rubbish!) (Picture four.)

Vocabulary

balloon   bin   grass   road   rubbish   traffic lights

61

Review

1 🔊 💬 Listen and say the letter.

a   b   c

d   e   f

2 🔍 💬 Read and answer.

Nick and Tony are at the farm. They're looking at the  🫏 . Next to the donkey there are three 🦆 . They're eating 🥖 . A 🐸 is 🧒 . Tony's very 😊 .

1. Where is Nick?
2. What are they looking at?
3. How many ducks are there?
4. What's the frog doing?

3 Play the game. Answer the question.

"Where's the star?" "It's in front of the pet shop."

9 Our clothes

1 🎧 CD3 8 💬 Listen and answer.

- sunglasses
- shirt
- jeans
- hat
- glasses
- handbag
- dress

2 🎧 CD3 9 💬 Listen and repeat.

3 Listen and point. Chant.

Handbags, glasses,
Jackets and shirts.
T-shirts, trousers,
Dresses and skirts.
Hats, jeans,
Shoes and socks.
Put them on,
They're in the box.

4 Listen and correct.

There's a big box with toys.

No, there's a big box with clothes.

Vocabulary
dress   glasses   handbag   hat   jeans   shirt

5 🔊 Listen and point.

"I've got a big car. Have you got a car, Trevor?"

"No, I haven't."

6 🔊 Listen and repeat.

Grammar

Have you got … ?   Yes, I have.   No, I haven't.
Has he/she got … ?   Yes, he/she has.   No, he/she hasn't.

7 🎵 Listen and point. Sing.

I've got a big garden,
I've got a big house.
I've got a good friend,
A small toy mouse.
I've got you, Monty.
I've got you.

Oh, Marie!

I've got a black mask,
And a big blue car.
I've got black glasses,
I'm the Maskman star,
And I've got you, Monty.
I've got you.

Oh, Maskman!

I haven't got
Superhero clothes.
I've got purple hair,
And a big green nose,
And I've got you, Monty.
I've got you.

Oh, Trevor!

I've got you, Monty.
I've got you.

8 💬 Ask and answer.

(Have you got a garden?)   (Yes, I have.)

9 Monty's phonics

7 seven

sheep

shop

Seven sheep are sleeping in a shop!

10 Ask and answer.

Ben: Has Ben got shorts?

No, he hasn't.

a   b   c   d

11 **Listen to the story.**

1 — Monty! Are you wearing my long white jacket and my glasses?
— Yes, I am. I'm Marie Mouse.

2 — Trevor! What are you wearing?
— I'm wearing blue trousers, a blue shirt, a blue hat and a black mask. Who am I?

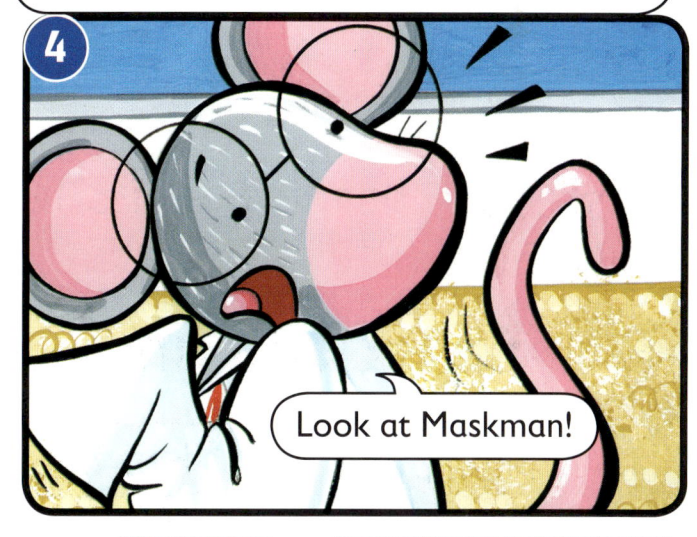

3 I can swim and fly, but I can't sing or dance. I'm … Masktroll!

4 Look at Maskman!

5 — Maskman! Are you eating a pencil?
— Yes, I am. Who am I?

6 — You're … Trollman!
— That's right! I can't swim and I can't spell.
— No, you can't, Trollman, but you've got a lot of friends.

12 **Listen and say the number.**

10 Our hobbies

1 🎧 CD3 22 💬 Listen and answer.

- badminton
- table tennis
- painting
- hockey
- basketball
- baseball

Sports

2 🎧 CD3 23 💬 Listen and repeat.

3 Listen and match. Say the hobby.

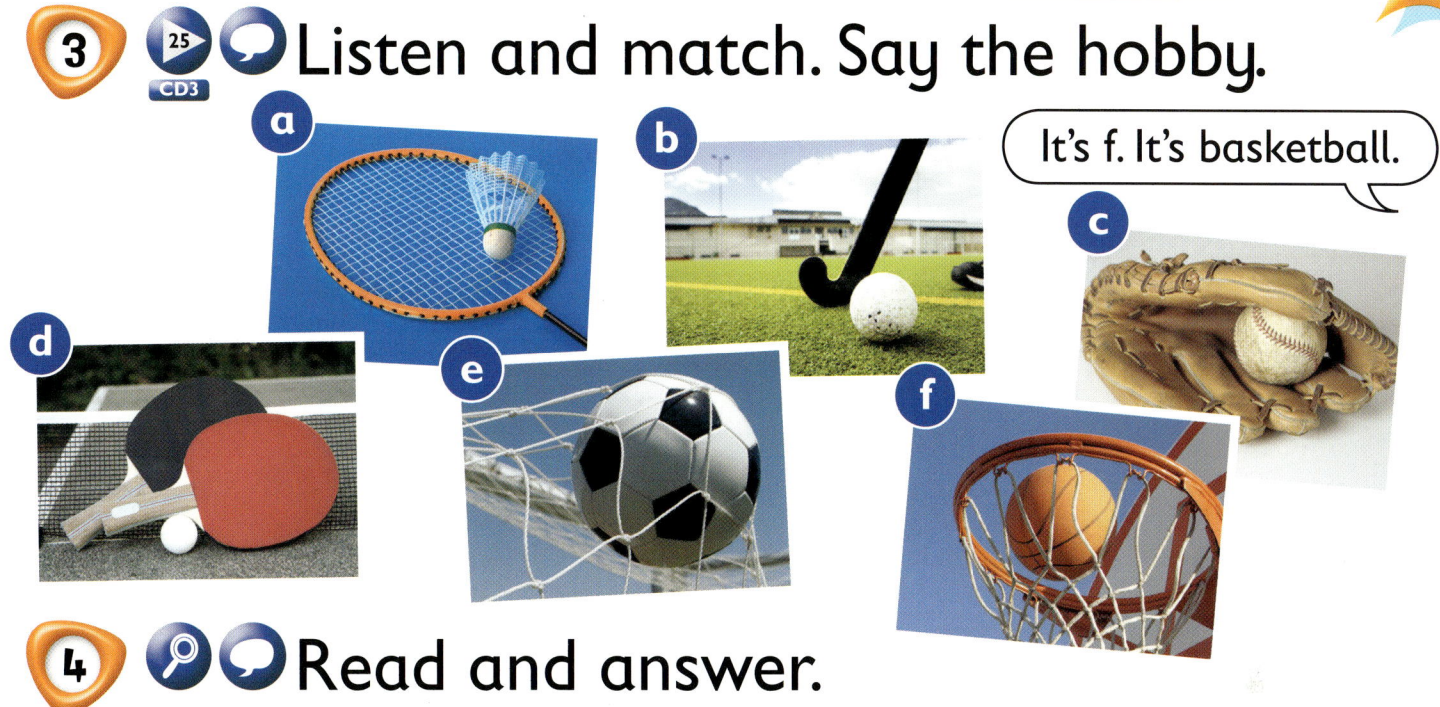

a b c d e f

It's f. It's basketball.

4 Read and answer.

These children are playing football. This sport has got two names: football and soccer. In a football team, there are ten players who can run and kick the ball, and one player who can kick and catch the ball. This player is the goalkeeper. Can you see the goalkeeper in this picture? She's wearing an orange T-shirt, black shorts and yellow boots.

1. The children are playing
   a) badminton.
   b) basketball.
   c) football.

2. Eleven players can
   a) kick the ball.
   b) catch the ball.
   c) bounce the ball.

3. One player can
   a) run.
   b) hit the ball.
   c) catch the ball.

Vocabulary
paint   play badminton/baseball/basketball/hockey/table tennis

5 Listen and say the number. *Number three.*

1
Name: Grandpa Star
Likes: fishing and badminton
Dislikes: cleaning his shoes

2
Name: Lenny
Likes: swimming and football
Dislikes: table tennis

3
Name: Mr Star
Likes: the guitar and cooking
Dislikes: horses

4
Name: Grandma Star
Likes: painting and driving
Dislikes: gardening

5
Name: Meera
Likes: bikes and photos
Dislikes: TV

6
Name: Alex
Likes: badminton and the piano
Dislikes: baseball

7
Name: Simon
Likes: basketball and hockey
Dislikes: cleaning his room

8
Name: Mrs Star
Likes: horses and reading
Dislikes: cooking

9
Name: Suzy
Likes: singing and drawing
Dislikes: soccer

10
Name: Stella
Likes: the piano and reading
Dislikes: doing sport

Grammar
I like / love …ing.   I don't like …ing.

6 🎵 Listen and point. Sing.

I ♥♥ fishing,
I ♥♥ flying kites,
I ♥ taking photos,
I ♥ riding bikes.
I ♥♥ fishing!
Bedum ... bedoo.

I ♥♥ swimming,
Playing hockey too,
And I ♥♥ painting,
With the colour blue.
I ♥♥ swimming!
Bedum ... bedoo.

I ✘ driving,
Or flying in a plane,
I ✘ cleaning shoes,
I ✘ running for a train!
Bedum ... bedoo.

I ✘ cooking,
Or playing the guitar,
I ✘ badminton,
Or cleaning my dad's car.
I ✘ it!
Bedum ... bedoo.

7 💬 Ask and answer.

Does Simon like painting?

Yes, he does.

8 Monty's phonics

king

sing

morning

The ki**ng** si**ng**s in the morni**ng**.

9 Ask your friend.

1. Do you like playing basketball?
2. Do you like reading?
3. Do you like fishing?
4. Do you like playing tennis?
5. Do you like painting?
6. What's your favourite hobby?

Do you like playing basketball?

No, I don't.

10 🎧 Listen to the story.

1. What a great game of soccer! Yes! What a great goal!

2. Number 18 is kicking the ball. Now number 15 is hitting the ball with his head.

3. Ouch! My hands!
No, Maskman! You can't touch the ball with your hands!

4. Now number 15 is running with the ball …

5. Trevor! Are you eating the ball?
No, I'm not.

6. Come and play football with us, Marie!
Oh no, boys! I love reading about soccer, but I don't like playing it.

11 🎧 💬 Listen and say 'yes' or 'no'.

Marie's maths — Venn diagrams

1 Ask and answer.

"What's this?"
"It's a sheep."

Wool   We wear...

2 Listen and say.

"It's wool. It's a toy. What is it?"
"It's a doll."

Vocabulary: wool

Now you! Activity Book page 76

Sports rules | Trevor's values

3 🎧 💬 Listen and say the number.

1
2
3
4

4 💬 Ask and answer.

— You can hit the ball with bats. Which sport is it?
— Table tennis.

Vocabulary
bounce   stick   bat

11 My birthday

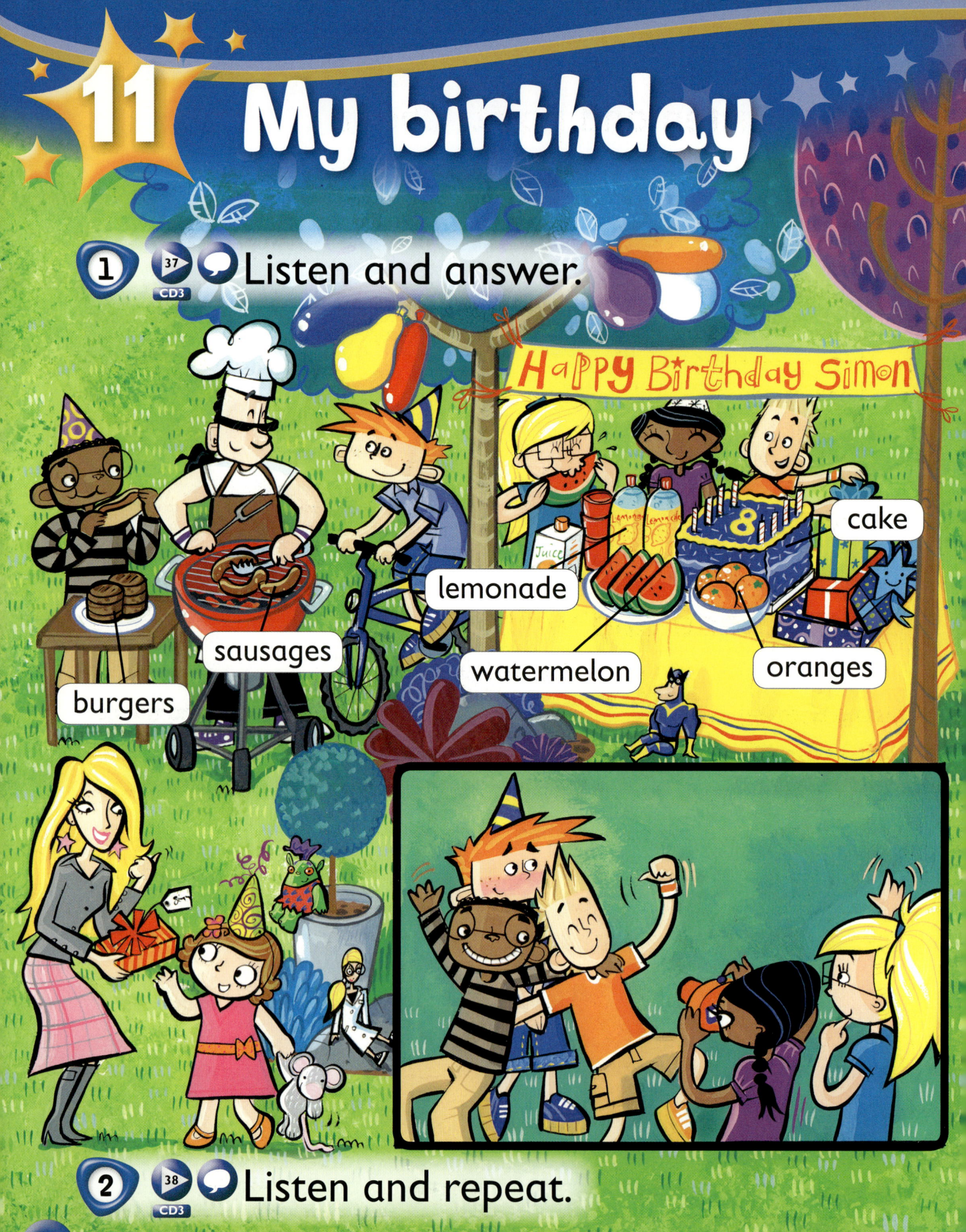

1 🎧 CD3 37 💬 Listen and answer.

Happy Birthday Simon

- cake
- lemonade
- oranges
- watermelon
- sausages
- burgers

2 🎧 CD3 38 💬 Listen and repeat.

3 Listen and point. Chant.

Look at them
Five young men.
Look at him
He can swim.
Look at her
In her new skirt.
Look at you
And your nice clean shoe.
Look at us
On a big red bus.
Look at me
I'm under a tree.

4 Read and write.

Birthday party

It is my birthday ___party___ this afternoon. Mum and Dad are doing things in the house. Mum is in the living room, standing on a **1** _____ . She is putting some green, blue, and purple **2** _____ on the wall and on the door. Dad is making some mango ice cream in the **3** _____ . There is some food and lots of **4** _____ on the table. My birthday **5** _____ has chocolate and fruit in it.

Example

party 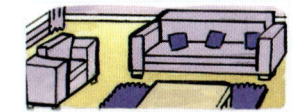   living room    balloons    kitchen

drinks    cake    shoes    chair

Vocabulary

burger   cake   lemonade   orange   sausage   watermelon

5 🎧 CD3 41 💬 Listen and answer.

Would you like some fries?

Yes, I'd love some.

6 🎧 CD3 42 💬 Listen and repeat.

Grammar
Would you like …?   Can I have …?   Here you are.

7 🔊 🎵 Listen and point. Sing.

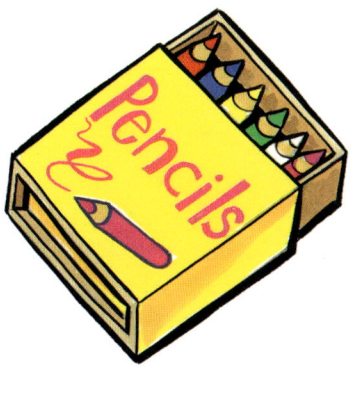

I'd like a great big chocolate cake,
And I'd like one for me.
I'd like a nice long sausage,
And I'd like one for me.

I'd like a burger and some fries,
And I'd like some for me.
I'd like a drink of lemonade,
And I'd like some for me.

I'd like coloured pencils, ...
I'd like a box of coloured pencils,

Don't give any to me!

8 💬 Ask and answer.

Would you like a burger?   Yes, please.   No, thank you.

9 Monty's phonics

purple

bird

girl

A purple bird for the birthday girl!

10 Look at the menu. Ask and answer.

Menu

Food
- burger
- sausages
- meatballs
- fish
- fries
- tomatoes
- carrots

Drinks
- lemonade
- orange juice
- milk
- water

What would you like to eat?

I'd like a burger and fries, please.

And what would you like to drink?

I'd like orange juice, please.

11 **Listen to the story.**

1. It's Marie's birthday today. Let's have a party for Marie! Let's make her a pencil cake. No, Trevor. Marie would like a lemon cake.

2. Let's have burgers and fries to eat. No, Maskman. It isn't your birthday.

3. Now let's make the cake.

4. Ssh. Marie's coming! Now we can't make her a cake.

5. Happy birthday, Marie!

6. Thanks, boys! Would you like to come to the café with me? Can I have some pencil cake, please?

12 **Act out the story.**

12 On holiday!

1 🎵 Listen and point.

mountain

sun
beach
sea
shell
sand

2 💬 Listen and repeat.

3 🎵 Listen and point. Sing.

I'm writing a new song,
I'm writing a new song.
At the beach, at the beach.

Suzy's getting lots of shells,
She's getting lots of shells.
At the beach, at the beach.

Simon's swimming in the sea,
Simon's swimming in the sea.
At the beach, at the beach.

Dad's walking on the sand,
Dad's walking on the sand.
At the beach, at the beach.

Mum's reading in the sun,
Mum's reading in the sun.
At the beach, at the beach ...

4 💬 Ask and answer.

What's Stella doing?   She's writing a song.

Vocabulary
beach   mountain   sand   sea   shell   sun

5 Listen and answer.

Do you want to go to a big city?

Where do you want to go on holiday?

I want to go to the mountains.

Grammar
Do you want to …?   I want to …   I don't want to …

6 Listen and point. Chant.

I want a 🎩

And you want some 👖.

She wants some 🥔

And he wants some 🫛.

They want a 🐑

And we want a 🐐.

She wants a 🚙

And he wants a ⛵.

7 Listen and say the letter.

Which melon do you want?   I want the big green one.   That's m.

8 Monty's phonics

Mum Dad

Ben Jill

Tom

Mum, Dad, Ben, Jill, and Tom are on the bus.

9 Ask and answer.

Do you like fishing?

No, I don't.

10 🔊 Listen to the story.

1. Here we are in the mountains.
Look, I've got a postcard from Maskman.

2. Listen. 'Hello. I'm at the beach. It's beautiful. I love sleeping in the sun and drinking lemonade …

3. I want to go to 'Star Beach' and see Maskman.
OK, Trevor. We can go and find Maskman.

4. Hmm … I want my new dress, my new shoes … and my new sunhat and sunglasses.

5. I'm on holiday. Can you get me some lemonade, please, Metal Mouth?

6. Maskman! Is this 'Star Beach'?
Hello. Er, yes, it is.
Ha ha ha.

11 🔊 💬 Listen and say the number.

Marie's geography — Maps

1 🎧 💬 **Listen and answer.**

"Look at D1. What can you see?" "I can see mountains."

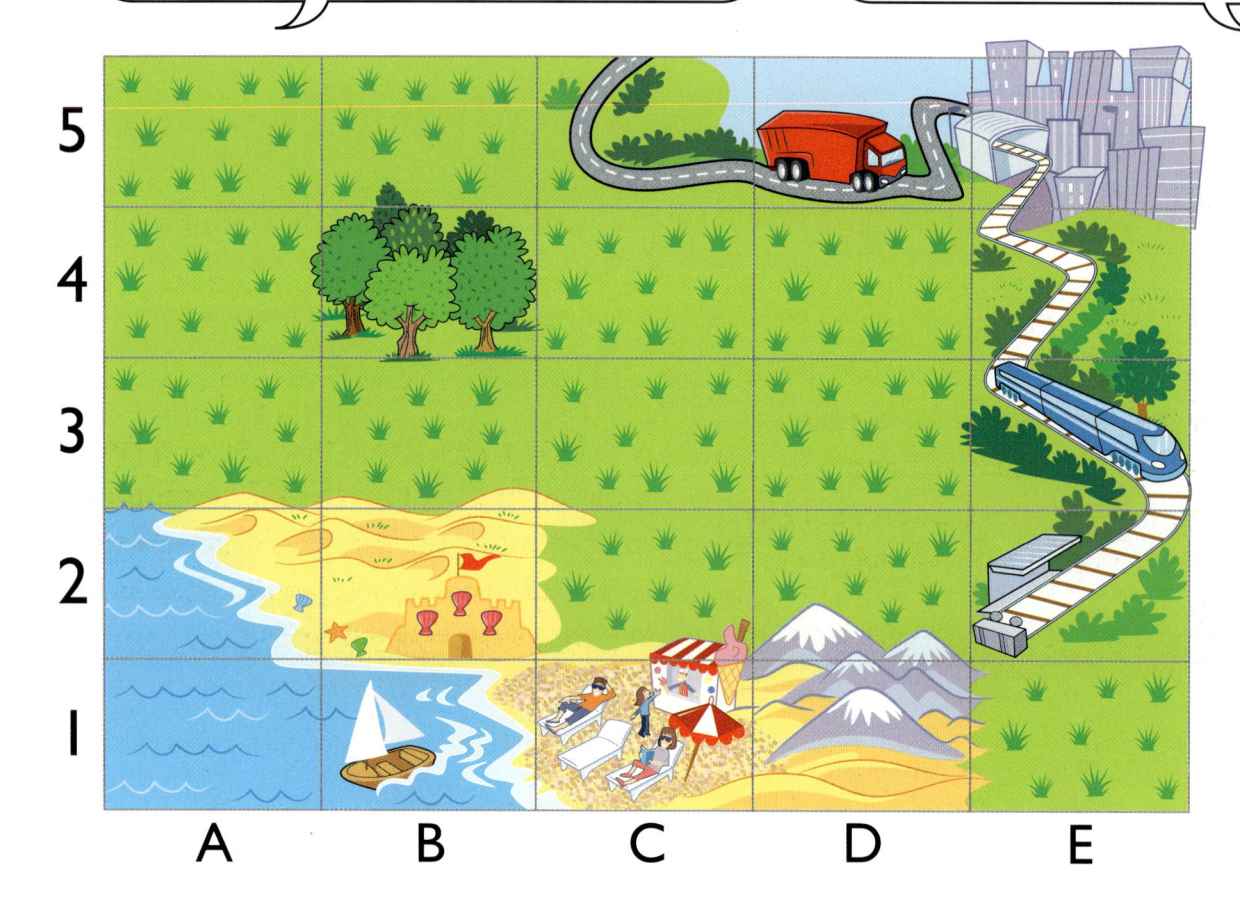

2 🔍 💬 **Play the game with a friend.**

"I can see mountains. Where am I?" "D1."

Now you!
Activity Book page 90

Helping holidays — Trevor's values

3 🔍 **Read and match.**

1 2 3

a

Hello
I'm Ben and I'm ten. I'm on holiday at an elephant park. It's cool! These elephants don't have a family. I clean the baby elephants and give them food.
I love animals!
Ben

b

Hello
I'm Miss Jones. I'm a teacher and I'm on holiday in the mountains. The mountains are beautiful and green. I'm teaching these children to speak with their hands. It's fun. We are very happy!
Sue

c

Hello
I'm Grace. I'm on holiday at the beach. The beach is black and dirty. The sea birds can't fly or swim. I'm cleaning the beach and the birds on the beach.
Grace

4 🔊 CD4 17 💬 **Listen and say 'yes' or 'no'.**

Grace's on holiday in the mountains.   No.

Review

1 🎧 💬 **Listen and correct.**

"The boy's wearing a green shirt."

"No, he's wearing a red shirt."

2 🔍 💬 **Look and say with a friend.**

"In picture one the woman's reading, but in picture two she's writing."

1

2

3 Play the game.

Red square – read and do
Blue square – What's this?
Green square – What's he / she doing?

Finish

Start

You've got your sunhat. Go forward 2 squares.

You haven't got your sunhat. Go back 2 squares.

Your kite hasn't got a tail. Go back 1 square.

The sea's dirty. Go back 2 squares.

The sea's clean. Go forward 2 squares.

93

Grammar reference

1

| Who's he? | This is my brother, Simon. He's seven. |
| Who's she? | This is my sister, Suzy. She's four. |

Who's he? = Who is he?   he's = he is   she's = she is

2

How many desks are there?	There are a lot of desks.
Is there a whiteboard on the wall?	Yes, there is. / No, there isn't.
Are there 10 desks in the classroom?	Yes, there are. / No, there aren't.

there's = there is   there aren't = there are not

3

| Whose is this camera? | It's Simon's. |
| Whose are these books? | They're Suzy's. |

It's Simon's. = It's Simon's camera.
They're Suzy's. = They're Suzy's books.

4

Whose is that green T-shirt?	It's mine.
Whose socks are those?	They're yours.
Is that dress yours, Suzy?	Yes, it is. / No, it isn't.
Are those socks yours, Simon?	Yes, they are. / No, they aren't.

It's mine. = It's my T-shirt.   No, they aren't. = No, they are not.

5

I'm He's / She's You're / They're / We're	singing. not flying.
What are you doing, Suzy? What's Grandpa doing?	

6

Can I have some meatballs, please?	Here you are.

7

I love donkeys.	So do I. / I don't.

8

Where's the park? Where are the flats?	It's They're	behind / in front of / next to the shops. behind / in front of / next to the shops.
Where's the school? Where are the shops?	It's They're	between the café and the park. between the café and the park.

9

He's / She's They're	wearing blue shorts and white shoes. wearing sunglasses and big hats.	
Have you Has he / she	got a watch?	Yes, I have. / No, I haven't. Yes, he / she has. No, he / she hasn't.

haven't got = have not got   hasn't got = has not got

10

I He / She	love / like / don't like loves / likes / doesn't like	swimming. playing table tennis.
Do you like reading?		Yes, I do. / No, I don't.

doesn't = does not

11

Would you like a burger? Would you like some lemonade?	Yes, please. No, thank you. I'd like some juice.

I'd like = I would like

12

Where do you want to go on holiday? Do you want to go to a big city?	I want to go to the mountains. I don't want to go to the beach.

Starters practice test
Listening
Reading & writing

Starters practice test — Listening

Part 1 5 questions

Listen and draw lines. There is one example.

Eva   Anna   Dan   Sam

Matt   Lucy   Nick

Part 2   5 questions

Read the question. Listen and write a name or a number.

There are two examples.

Examples

What is the boy's name? ....Mark............

How old is he? ....9............

Questions

1. Which class is Mark in now? ----------------------

2. What's Mark's family name? ----------------------

3. Where does Mark live? ---------------------- Street

4. What number is Mark's house? ----------------------

5. How many people live in Mark's house? ----------------------

Part 3 5 questions

Listen and tick (✓) the box. There is one example.
What can Sam have?

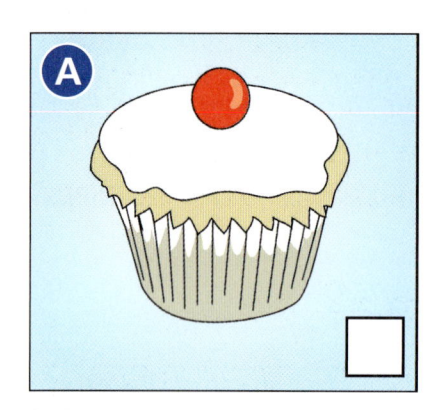

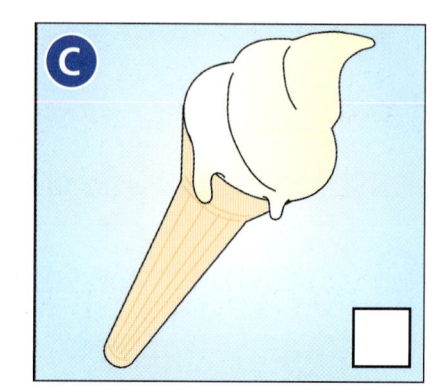

A [cupcake] ☐   B [carrot] ✓   C [ice cream] ☐

1 What does Anna want?

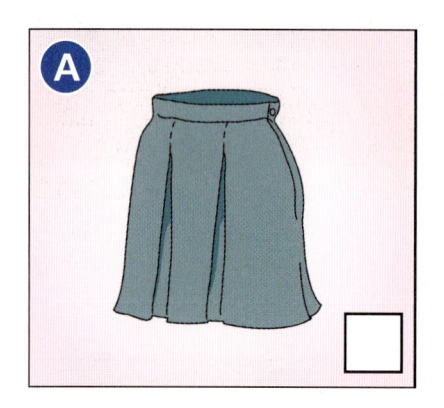

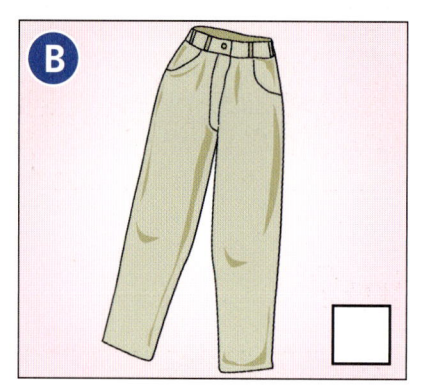

A [skirt] ☐   B [trousers] ☐   C [dress] ☐

2 What is Ben drawing?

A [cow] ☐   B [goat] ☐   C [sheep] ☐

3 What is Mum doing?

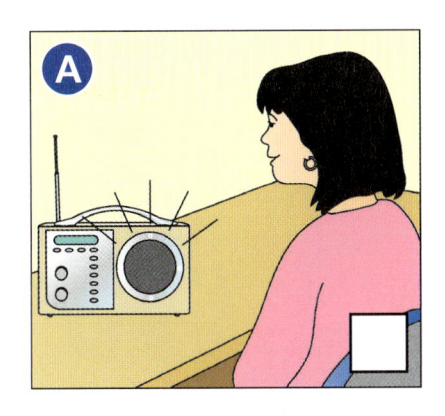

4 What is Mr Gray's favourite game?

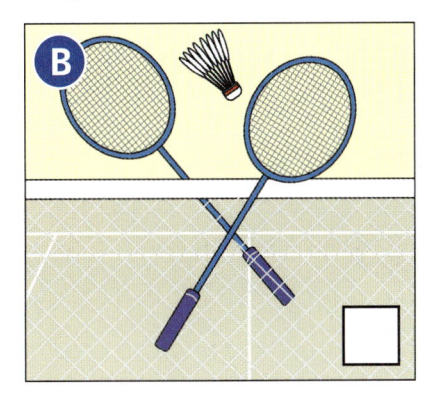

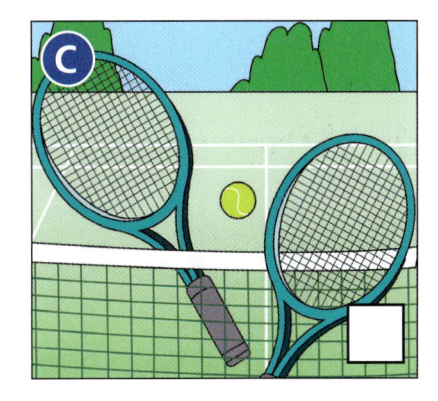

5 Which girl is Kim?

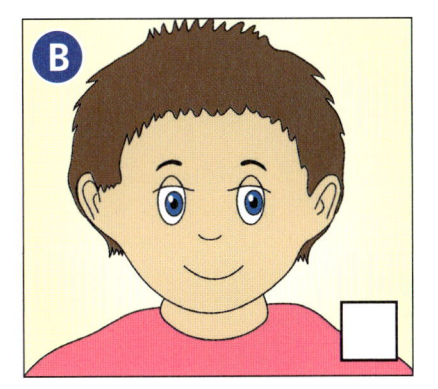

Part 4   5 questions

Listen and colour. There is one example.

Starters practice test   Reading & writing

Part 1   5 questions

Look and read. Put a tick (✓) or a cross (✗) in the box.

There are two examples.

Examples

This is a car. ✓

These are rulers. ✗

Questions

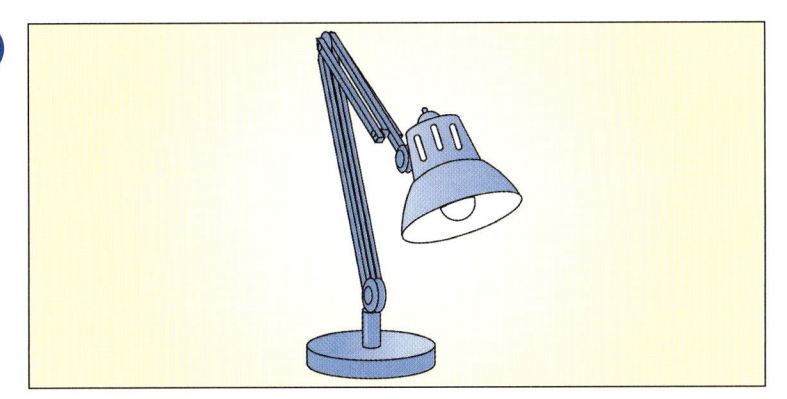

1

This is a lamp. ☐

2 These are mangoes. ☐

3 This is a jacket. ☐

4 This is a piano. ☐

5 This is a robot. ☐

Part 2 5 questions

Look and read. Write yes or no.

Examples

A girl is kicking a football.   yes

Two children have got kites.   no

Questions

1. The boys are riding bikes.   _____
2. There are two ducks in the water.   _____
3. The woman is painting a picture.   _____
4. The baby is playing with a doll.   _____
5. The man has got a black dog.   _____

Part 3 5 questions

Look at the pictures. Look at the letters.
Write the words.

Example

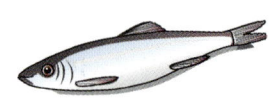

f i s h

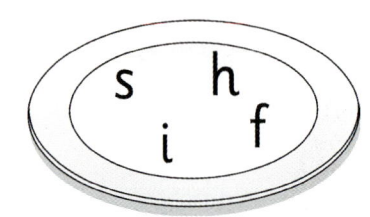

Questions

1. _ _ _ _ _  
2. _ _ _ _ _  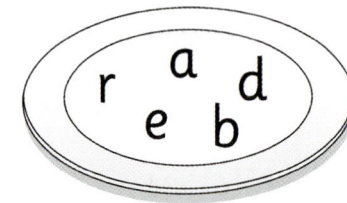
3. _ _ _ _ _ _  
4. _ _ _ _ _ _  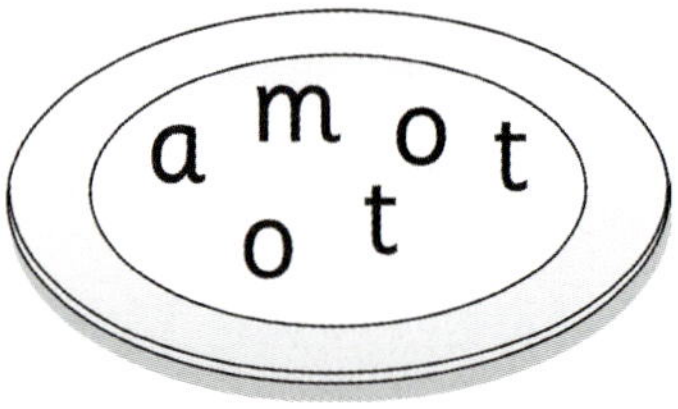
5. _ _ _ _ _ _ _

Part 4 5 questions

Read this. Choose a word from the box. Write the correct word next to numbers 1–5. There is one example.

A bird

I'm a small animal. I've got two ……… legs ……… , but I haven't got (1) ……………………… . I've got a short (2) ……………………… . I can fly and I live in a big (3) ……………………… in the garden. In the morning I sing beautiful songs. I like eating (4) ……………………… and small animals like spiders. (5) ……………………… like me a lot, but I don't like them!

| legs | fruit | cats | flower |
| arms | plane | tail | tree |

Part 5   5 questions

Look at the pictures and read the questions.
Write one-word answers.

Examples

Who is having breakfast?   a _____boy_____

How many books has the boy got?   _____three_____

Questions

1 What is the boy's mother
pointing to?   the _____

2) What is the boy doing? ....

3) Where are the girls? on the ....

4) What is the boy doing now? ....

5) Who looks angry? the ....

Thanks and Acknowledgements

Authors' thanks

Many thanks to everyone at Cambridge University Press and in particular to:

Rosemary Bradley for supervising the whole project and for her keen editorial eye;
Emily Hird for her energy, enthusiasm and enormous organisational capacity;
Claire Appleyard for all her hard work and sound contributions;
Colin Sage for his good ideas and helpful suggestions;
Karen Elliot for her enthusiasm and creative reworking of the Phonics sections.

We would also like to thank all our pupils and colleagues at Star English, El Palmar, Murcia and especially Jim Kelly and Julie Woodman for their help and suggestions at various stages of the project.

Dedications

I would like to dedicate this book to the women who have been my pillars of strength: Milagros Marín, Sara de Alba, Elia Navarro and Maricarmen Balsalobre - CN

To Paloma, for her love, encouragement and unwavering support. Thanks. - MT

The Authors and Publishers would like to thank the following teachers for their help in reviewing the material and for the invaluable feedback they provided:

Alice Matovich, Cecilia Sanchez, Florencia Durante, Maria Loe Antigona, Argentina; Erica Santos, Brazil; Ma Xin, Ren Xiaochi, China; Albeiro Monsalve Marin, Colombia; Agata Jankiewicz, Poland; Maria Antonia Castro, Spain; Catherine Taylor, Turkey.

The authors and publishers would like to thank the following consultants for their invaluable feedback:

Coralyn Bradshaw, Pippa Mayfield, Hilary Ratcliff, Melanie Williams.

We would also like to thank all the teachers who allowed us to observe their classes, and who gave up their invaluable time for interviews and focus groups.

The authors and publishers acknowledge the following sources of copyright material and are grateful for the permissions granted. While every effort has been made, it has not always been possible to identify the sources of all the material used, or to trace all copyright holders. If any omissions are brought to our notice, we will be happy to include the appropriate acknowledgements on reprinting.

t = top, c = centre, b = below, l = left, r = right

p.16 (orange): Shutterstock/Maks Narodenko; p.16 (banana): Shutterstock/brulove; p.16 (apple): Shutterstock/Roman Samokhin; p.16 (pear): Shutterstock/Andrey Eremin; p.16 (pineapple): Shutterstock/Alex Staroseltsev; p.16 (lemon): Shutterstock/topseller; p.17 (t): Thinkstock; p.31 (t): Thinkstock; p.31 (1): Thinkstock/iStockphoto; p.31 (2): Shutterstock/Sergey Karpov; p.31 (3): Shutterstock/Aron Brand; p.31 (4): Shutterstock/Feng Yu; p.31 (bl): Shutterstock/Picsfive; p.31 (bc): Shutterstock/Skylines; p.31 (br): Shutterstock/Quang Ho; p.32 (11): Shutterstock/Iwona Grodzka; p.32 (12): Shutterstock/K. Miri Photography; p.32 (13): Shutterstock/DenisNata; p.32 (14): Shutterstock/Luis Carlos Torres; p.32 (15): Shutterstock/Masalski Maksim; p.32 (16): Shutterstock/terekhov igor; p.32 (17): Shutterstock/Nikuwka; p.32 (18): Alamy/Graham Morley; p.32 (19): Alamy/Mike Stone; p.32 (20): Shutterstock/Mostphotos; p.46 (tl): Alamy/Christine Whitehead; p.46 (tc): Shutterstock/Paul Cowan; p.46 (tr): Shutterstock/Nattika; p.46 (bl): Shutterstock/Diana Taliun; p.46 (bc): Shutterstock/Nattika; p.46 (br): Shutterstock/Maks Narodenko; p.47 (t): Thinkstock; p.60 (1): Shutterstock/agrosse; p.60 (2): Shutterstock/IbajaUsap; p.60 (3): Shutterstock/ Aleksandr Kurganov; p.60 (4): Shutterstock/Eduard Kyslynskyy; p.60 (5): Shutterstock/Menno Schaefer; p.60 (6): Shutterstock/ mexrix; p.61 (t): Thinkstock; p.71 (a): iStockphoto/valda; p.71 (b): istockphoto/RapidEye; p.71 (c): istockphoto/TAPshooter; p.71 (d): istockphoto/valdecasas; p.71 (e): istockphoto/padnpen; p.71 (f): istockphoto/Oksana Struk; p.76 (wool): Shutterstock/OlyaSenko; p.76 (tl): Shutterstock/Againstar; p.76 (tc): Shutterstock/Karkas; p.76 (tr): Shutterstock/tarasov; p.76 (cl): Shutterstock/Eric Isselee; p.76 (c): Shutterstock/Mitrofanova; p.76 (cr): Shutterstock/Ruslan Kudrin; p.76 (bl): Shutterstock/LeshaBu; p.76 (bc): Shutterstock/Maksym Bondarchuk ; p.76 (br): Getty Images/iStock/windujedi; p.77 (t): Thinkstock; p.91 (t): Thinkstock; p.91 (1): GettyImages/SolStock/E+; p.91 (2): Corbis/Richard T. Nowitz; p.91 (3): GettyImages/Cavan Images.

Commissioned photography on pages 7, 8, 14, 22, 28, 30, 35, 38, 44, 52, 58, 74, 82, 88, 90 by Trevor Clifford Photography.

Sound recordings p60, CD2, track 3: *Jelly & Icecream 3* by Gleddon/Loy/Bussey. Copyright © Audio Network Limited; Ottoman Sands by Panayi. Copyright © Audio Network Limited; *Spider's web* by Tom Smail. Copyright © Audio Network Limited; Saint Saens - *Carnival of the Animals No 10 (Aviary)*, Saint Saens - *Carnival of the Animals No 7 (Aquarium)*, and Rossini - *William Tell Overture* (trumpet entry). Licensed by http://www.royaltyfreeclassicalmusic.co.uk

The authors and publishers are grateful to the following illustrators:

Andrew Hennessey; jon Batton, c/oBeehive; Beatrice Costamagna, c/o Pickled ink; Chris Garbutt, c/o Arena; Lucía Serrano Guerroro; Andrew Hennessey; Kelly Kennedy, c/o Syvlie Poggio; Bethan Matthews, c/o Sylvie Poggio; Rob McKlurkan, c/o The Bright Agency; Melanie Sharp, c/o Syvlie Poggio; Marie Simpson, c/o Pickled ink; Emily Skinner, c/o Graham-Cameron Illustration; Lisa Smith; Gary Swift; Lisa Williams, c/o Sylvie Poggio

The publishers are grateful to the following contributors:

Louise Edgeworth: picture research and art direction
Wild Apple Design Ltd: page design
Blooberry: additional design
Lon Chan: cover design
Melanie Sharp: cover illustration
John Green and Tim Woolf, TEFL Audio: audio recordings
Robert Lee: song writing
hyphen S.A.: editorial management